• HALSGROVE DISCOVER SERIES ➤

THE YORKSHIRE RIVER DERWENT

Moments in Time

DEDICATION

To the memory of

Pete Bowler
Eleanor Burnett
Mike Clegg
The Viscount Downe
Allen Edwards MBE
Cedric Flynn
Michael Gregory
David Hall
Ginny Knowlson
Phil Lester
Freddy Proctor
Geoff Smith
Stephen Warburton

'little streams' who, each in their own sometimes unseen ways,
influenced the course of the Derwent's history, and who passed too soon.

• HALSGROVE DISCOVER SERIES ➤

THE YORKSHIRE RIVER DERWENT

Moments in Time

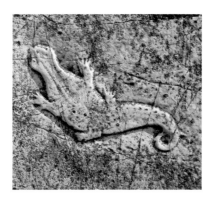

IAN CARSTAIRS

HALSGROVE
In association with The Light Owler Trust

Acknowledgements

Many thousands of people and large numbers of organisations and groups have played a part in the conservation of the Yorkshire River Derwent. It would be invidious to mention some, for by so doing I would inevitably leave out many others who would deserve equal mention. In Final Word on page 139 I have included a tribute to them all. Special thanks is, however, due here to my wife Jan and parents, Teresa and Archer, for their enduring support for the cause, in all its shapes and forms, over the years.

The photographs are by the author, except as follows.
Neil Mitchell, APS (UK): 39 bottom left, 48 top left, 58, 88, 108 top left, 119 bottom left, 120 left, 127 right.
North York Moors National Park Authority: 21 top centre.

Conventions

Numerous organisations, some of which have changed their names are central to the Derwent's story. The first time an organisation is mentioned within a chapter its title is set out in full, thereafter for brevity only initials are used. Where organisations have changed their name, the current one at the time of the event described is used. A reference list of abbreviations and name changes is shown on page 143.

Frontispiece photograph: *An 'Aske' – a local name for a newt – carved into the stonework of All Saint's Church, Aughton to commemorate Robert Aske, who was executed by Henry VIII for his part in the Pilgrimage of Grace.*

First published in Great Britain in 2007

Copyright © 2007 Ian Carstairs

British Library Cataloguing-in-Publication Data

A CIP record for this title is available from the British Library

ISBN 978 1 84114 567 9

HALSGROVE
Halsgrove House, Ryelands Industrial Estate,
Bagley Road, Wellington, Somerset TA21 9PZ
Tel: 01823 653777   Fax: 01823 216796
email: sales@halsgrove.com
website: www.halsgrove.com

Printed and bound by Grafiche Flaminia, Italy

Contents

Preface by Professor Sir John Lawton   7
Foreword by Chris Yates   9
Introduction – First Sight   11

A CLASSIC RIVER
Chapter One   *Up in the Hills*   19
Chapter Two   *Down the Valleys*   27
Chapter Three   *Through the Middle Reaches*   37
Chapter Four   *Across the Floodplain*   45

MOMENTS IN TIME
Chapter Five   *Barrage of Criticism*   55
Chapter Six   *Purchase and Protect*   63
Chapter Seven   *Challenges in Court*   71
Chapter Eight   *Getting an Act Together*   77
Chapter Nine   *Battle of the Evidence*   85
Chapter Ten   *Highs and Lows*   93
Chapter Eleven   *A River Defined*   99
Chapter Twelve   *The Ripple Effect*   105
Chapter Thirteen   *Sense of Place*   111
Chapter Fourteen   *Coal Comfort*   117
Chapter Fifteen   *Sowing Seeds*   125
Chapter Sixteen   *Handing on the Baton*   131

Final Word – The Ever-rolling Stream   139
Post Script   142

Preface

By *Professor Sir John Lawton CBE FRS*

Since childhood I've kept a natural history diary. The entry for 19th February 1974 reads: "Aughton church. Cold. 63 Bewick's swans, several thousand wigeon. 1 great grey shrike. Magic place!" That was my first close encounter with the Lower Derwent Valley.

I had moved to York in 1971, but the demands of a new job, family and house meant that opportunities to go birding were severely limited. Since that first visit, which is still vivid in my mind, I must have visited the Lower Derwent hundreds of times. I am less familiar with the river's upper reaches, but I know the whole catchment well enough now to appreciate just what a wonderful, unique part of England it is.

My working life has taken me to every continent in the world, and I have been hugely privileged to see some wonderful places and their wildlife. But I know of nowhere like the Derwent Valley. It is not just the wildlife, special as that is. It is scenically very beautiful, with landscapes steeped in history and moulded by man for millennia – moors, meadows and mediaeval churches strung like jewels along the winding river.

We have lost so much of Britain's wildlife and historic landscapes. Those areas that remain are priceless, not as museums frozen in time, but classrooms to show us how we can live and work in harmony with nature, and to enrich our lives.

Treasure this place. It is very special.

John Lawton
York

Opposite: *The River Derwent near Wheldrake Ings*

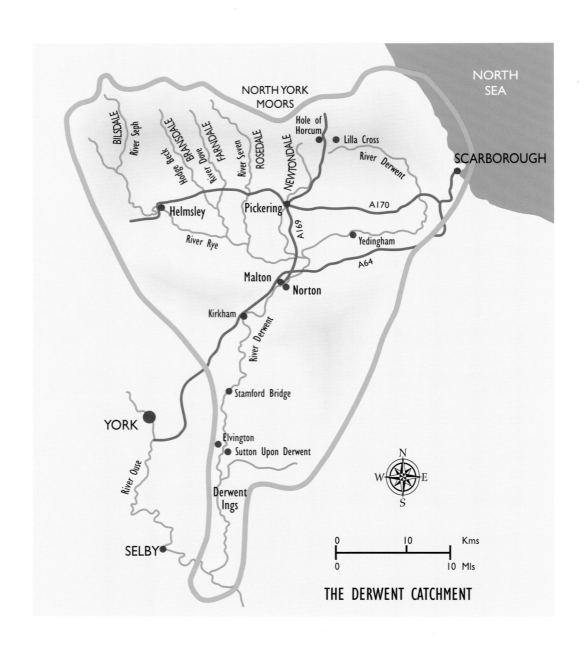

THE DERWENT CATCHMENT

Foreword

By Chris Yates GSC

It's very fortunate there are people on this earth like Ian, the author of this book. Hardly a day passes without us hearing of some lovely or unique part of the country being threatened by the demand for change. Usually we read or hear about each potential tragedy with nothing more than a resigned sigh, but every so often, something happens to drive us wild and make us say: 'Enough!' Then a campaigning zeal overcomes our normally quiescent nature and woe-betide those poor unfortunates who'd cast a shadow over some favourite part of our landscape. However, by teatime, when we realise we'll never raise the army we need to support our cause, we slide back into simmering regret which we might express by writing a letter to a newspaper. But, as I said, it's lucky there are individuals like Ian, people who not only have the desire to protect our natural heritage, but also possess the organisational skills and the sheer doggedness to be able to mount an effective response or generate a positive result.

Ian was a bit like a one-man environmental protection agency long before he joined up with others to raise the banner in the battle to save one of Britain's best rivers. Such was the challenge of this threat – a plan to transform the wilder reaches of the Yorkshire Derwent into a boating channel – it needed the combined skills of these dedicated people, all of similar mould, yet each with a specialist knowledge or particular connection with the river itself and who loved it for what it was. It was a happy coincidence (there are a number of other happy coincidences throughout this book) that the group came together when it did.

I have known Ian since our teenage years. We met in 1968, when we were at art school, and, probably because of his Scottish roots, he invited me to join his pipe band. In those early years I could never have imagined that my pal would become a saviour of the countryside, honoured by the Queen, yet even then I was always impressed by his commitment to whatever cause we happened to align ourselves with. And one of the reasons he was often successful in achieving his goals was simply because of his *appreciation* of those he had to convince. Ian believes in empathy. This is, I think, his secret weapon, and as this chronicle reveals, it works very effectively when he's championing one of the most important causes of all.

Chris Yates
Wiltshire

Overleaf: *At the northern end of Kirkham Gorge.*

Introduction

First Sight.

"So the river is a god

Knee-deep among reeds, watching men,
Or hung by the heels down the door of a dam

It is a god and inviolable"

Part of a poem published in support of the River Derwent in the summer of 1985,
by express permission of the late Ted Hughes, Poet Laureate.

I discovered the Yorkshire River Derwent, quite by accident one autumn day in the early 1970s while looking for badger setts. I had left the car near the Scrayingham road, crossed a field, slithered down a bank under massive beech trees and found myself beside this secret river, not far from Buttercrambe. It was heaven. The sun flickered through the overhanging boughs, insects danced over the shining slow-moving water and buzzed in the sheltered warmth.

I have no doubt I was trespassing; I didn't mean to, I was simply carried along with the mood of a fabulous moment in a wonderful place on a beautiful English afternoon. It was an experience which has stayed with me over the years, driving me on to play a part, with many others, in the constant challenge to protect the character of the river and render its future a little more secure; each trying in our own ways to hold a line in a wider countryside constantly under pressure for change.

On the bank I spotted a skeleton, lying undisturbed, as though the animal had fallen asleep and its flesh had been gently spirited away. Remarkable really, you'd have expected a crow or two, or perhaps a fox to have found the body and rearranged the pieces as they ate. But nothing seemed to have touched it.

I picked up the skull of my 'first' Derwent Otter, and put it carefully in my pocket. To this day, I keep it as a memento, producing it as a talisman at times of threat to the river in support of whatever project we might be on. You see I, and others who share my enthusiasm for protecting this delightful place, believe in the value of omens, coincidences and lucky charms. This is not just meaning-

Kirkham Bridge, at the southern end of Kirkham Gorge in 1985.

less superstition; over the years they have proved to be very real and reassuring, as you will find out.

Later that day I encountered the river again. Still looking for signs of badgers, I worked up the side of a small hill where a copse sat neatly, like a beret on its summit. An ash wood stretched along the side of the valley behind the hill and across a pasture lay the river, curving towards a steep-sided gorge. In the wood, a magnificent sett, home to generations of badgers, spread across the woodland floor, right to the edge of the trees. With a beautiful view across the valley to the river, the badgers had chosen well. For me it would be ideal too, to return to sit in the dark and wait. And even if the badgers didn't emerge, it was certainly a good place to be.

Leaving the wood, I met a farm worker, who viewed me with grave suspicion. Enquiring who farmed the land, at least avoided the 'what are you doing here' question, and anyway, if I had permission I could return, free from the anxiety that I should not really be here. He directed me to a nearby farmhouse, where I met Colin and Jean Clarkson, their son Charles and his then girlfriend – and later-to-be wife – Andrea. It was my subsequent friendship with the Clarksons and their shared desire that things should not change which welded my love of the river.

With Colin's consent, I returned often to the wood, to savour this unspoilt rural place alongside the Derwent. Each visit was memorable, but one occasion, many years later, stands out from all of the rest.

It was New Year's Eve. Jan Knowlson my then partner was with me, carrying a bottle of wine and a couple of glasses to 'see-in' the New Year with the badgers. A bright moon silhouetted the waving branches and twigs of the trees. In the middle distance, it glinted off the water at a bend in the river. Avoiding the false bonhomie, communal kissing and hand-shaking of the overindulged party was an attractive proposition. But the wood at midnight is a very different place to a warm room in a pub or house. Rational explanation deserts you and uncertainty fills the air.

With three minutes to go, way out in the blackness, the first church bells rang in their early New Year. A minute later from another direction a second peal followed from further away. In all we heard five sets of bells, not one of them on time.

In an equally random way, Auld Lang Syne, carried on thin un-harmonious voices from unknown parties in unseen houses threaded across the darkness. In response, everywhere in the tree tops, rooks and the occasional crow added their raucous contribution to the midnight hour. Separated from our electrically-governed world, the wood, overlooking the river, seemed perfect, a very far cry from the events which would unfold in the coming years.

Not long after my first encounters with the river, I met the late Stephen Warburton, the then newly appointed Field Officer for the Yorkshire Naturalists Trust, and an indefatigable champion of the Derwent's cause. Here was a kindred spirit, noted for his amazing intellect and unrelenting dog-with-a-bone approach to pursuing issues in which he believed. He may have sometimes ruffled a few feathers along the way, but no-one could ever have doubted his commitment. Without him, the river's fortunes might well have run a far less satisfactory course; it is no overstatement to say that Stephen is to the Derwent what, for those who are in the know, the legendary William Bunting is to Thorne and Hatfield Moors.

It was Stephen's tireless effort and academic and literary skills, which, working with Sarah Priest (botanist), Joan Burnett (farmer) and Mike Clegg (Countryman, broadcaster and fisherman) among others saw the publication in 1978 by the Conservation Society of the Yorkshire Derwent (CONSYDER) of the definitive report *The Yorkshire Derwent – A Case for Conservation.*

The late Ted Hughes, writing in support of our endeavours to protect the Derwent at the time of the Court actions seeking to open up and develop the river for navigation, which arose in the 1980s, bemoaned the fact that there was not such a group as ours to support the river near where he lived in Devon, nor a publication which coherently set out a justification for its protection in the way that A Case for Conservation did.

Now jump fast-forward twenty years and two hundred miles to a very different scene from the riverside wood. I am near the Houses of Parliament with two colleagues, Paul Smith, a solicitor, and Tim Dixon. We are about to find out the answer to a very important question: what exactly is a river?

Surprisingly, in a millennium of recorded history, a River had never been legally defined. That was, until lunchtime on 5th of December 1991. Sitting on the top deck of a bus destined for Clapham as it passed over the River Thames on Westminster Bridge, we had an answer.

Inside a manila envelope in Paul's hand, a Judgment of five Law Lords spelt it out, and a ten-year legal battle over the Yorkshire River Derwent was effectively at an end.

The House of Lords Test Case, the culmination of an exhausting progress through the Chancery Division of the High Court and the Court of Appeal, centred on the meaning of a few simple words: was a river 'land covered with water'? Why, you might ask, was this so important? Suffice to say, it was a ruling with far-reaching implications for rivers throughout England and Wales, as well as, of course for the Yorkshire Derwent, widely regarded as one of the loveliest, unspoilt rivers in the country.

But the Law Reports of the Judgment give few clues as to what really lay behind the defence of the case; who were the people who fought it, their strength of feeling, and how and why they had gone to such extraordinary lengths? And perhaps equally importantly for the River Derwent, what happened next.

History generally overlooks the ordinary person. Witness how little we know about their daily lives and deeds in the past, while Kings and Queens, politicians, high-ranking military and the great and the good are remembered as if theirs is the only story that counts. It is no different today, when even quite significant events soon slip from society's collective memory.

The Yorkshire River Derwent – Moments in Time records a short period in the River's recent history – a little slice of its intriguing story. It is about the achievements of committed local people, the knowledge of which would otherwise be lost, described through my personal experience of events, places and connections that have touched me.

A short while before Stephen Warburton died of cancer in January 2004, we lamented to each other that we had never managed to write a book of our experiences during and after the Derwent Court Case. Well, here it is and I make no apology for drawing inspiration from *The River Derwent – A Case for Conservation*. Without it as a solid foundation, marshalling the arguments and engaging supporters when they were needed would have been a much harder task. I hope also that this sequel, 30 years on, will add weight to the claim, that the Derwent was and still is 'A Case for Conservation' in more than one sense of the word.

In many ways, this book is more like two books in one. The First Part, A Classic River, explores the Upper Derwent and its tributaries in the North York Moors, before tracing a snaking course across the Vale of Pickering, down Kirkham Gorge, into the Lower Derwent Valley and on through its final journey united with the rivers Ouse, Trent, Ancholme and Hull as The Humber, to Spurn Point and the North Sea. It also sets the scene for a chain of defining events, which have charted the river's conservation in recent years.

The Second Section, Moments in Time, begins where the River Derwent ends – the Barmby Tidal Barrage, perhaps the single most significant catalyst to a 35-year fight for the River, its wildlife and the quality of the countryside. Or was it the abandonment of the Farndale reservoir scheme, or behind that the thirst of Yorkshire for water which could be said truly to lie at the root of this story?

Ian Carstairs
Chairman, The Light Owler Trust
York, Spring 2007

NEVER IN HIS LIFE HAD HE SEEN A RIVER BEFORE — THIS SLEEK SINUOUS FULL — BODIED ANIMAL, CHASING AND CHUCKLING, GRIPPING THINGS WITH A GURGLE AND LEAVING THEM WITH A LAUGH, TO FLING ITSELF ON FRESH PLAYMATES THAT SHOOK THEMSELVES FREE, AND WERE CAUGHT AND HELD AGAIN. ALL WAS A-SHAKE AND A-SHIVER — GLINTS & GLEAMS AND SPARKLES, RUSTLE AND SWIRL CHATTER AND BUBBLE.

An extract from Wind in the Willows, *set in cast iron on the riverside path between Norton and Malton.*

Overleaf: An unusual July flood engulfs the hay meadows below the Escrick Moraine.

Page 18: Railway Street bridge and old warehouse buildings, Malton.

A CLASSIC RIVER

CHAPTER ONE

Up in the Hills

Rising on Fylingdales Moor, the infant River Derwent descends from the heather-clad uplands, threading past vast conifer forests and into tight valleys at the start of its extraordinary journey towards the sea.

Close to Malton bus station, a Victorian bridge carries Railway Street over the silt-laden River Derwent. From the bridge, you will see a modest river, in summer fringed with reeds, water lilies and the occasional flowering rush.

Until 1804, when a relief channel, known as the Sea Cut, was completed between Hackness and Scalby, north of Scarborough, to divert some of the flow to the North Sea in times of flood, almost all the water draining from the entire southern slopes of the North York Moors and the whole of the Vale of Pickering squeezed through this narrow space.

Today, despite the early 19th Century works, the effects are much the same. After heavy rains or melting snow in the Moors, the river's personality changes swiftly, rising rapidly in a few hours, as the product of hundreds of square miles of wetness head simultaneously for the sea.

Contemplating the river in the centre of Malton, it is hard to appreciate the scale of the Derwent's catchment from which the river is fed. But take the Whitby bus from Malton bus station and ask the driver to set you down at Eller Beck in the middle of the North York Moors and you will begin to get an idea.

Ten miles north of Malton, beyond Pickering, the Whitby Road begins a long climb. Arable fields give way to upland grazing until at the Hole of Horcum, a vast natural amphitheatre, the view opens out to a breathtaking moorland vista stretching unobstructed to the distant horizon.

Folklore recounts that an irascible giant, Wade, created the spectacular Hole of Horcum. In a fit of temper he is said to have scooped up a vast chunk of the earth and hurled it at his wife, simultaneously producing a huge hole where he grabbed the massive handful, and Blakey Topping, a conical-shaped hill a mile-and-a-half away, when he missed her. More mundanely, reality is that this vast depression owes its origins not to a single dramatic event, but to the relentless action of springs eroding away the rock strata over mind-numbing lengths of time.

At Eller Beck, a path leads up to the remote and lonely Lilla Cross. Except it isn't quite as lonely as at first it seems. Each year thousands of people trudge this rough moorland track as they follow the Lyke Wake Walk on its arduous 42 miles route from Osmotherley, or the exhausting 192 miles Coast-to-Coast Walk from St Bees Head in Cumbria, to Robin Hood's Bay.

Lilla Cross has a very odd neighbour. To the south-west, the great single grey block of Fylingdales Early Warning Station – technically described as a truncated pyramid – is one of the most ugly structures imaginable, especially in such a beautiful location. Built as a high-tech listening-post, connected to similar apparatus in Greenland and Alaska, its job is to detect in-coming ballistic missiles and relay an alert.

Fylingdales wasn't always so ugly. Previously, three massive white spheres - popularly called domes and known affectionately as 'The Golf balls'- sat in a line on the moor, in a rather pleasing arrangement. Approached on a foggy day, they possessed a mysterious quality and seemed to take on a changing colour depending on the quality of the light. I loved the golf balls, and felt a strange sense of loss to the landscape when they were demolished. And I know I was not alone.

Isn't it ironic? When Fylingdales Early Warning Station was built in the 1950s, loaded with cold-war purpose and secrecy, people hated the intrusion and impact on the moors. In time, many rather ignored what the domes represented and began to enjoy them for what they looked like, so much so that they became a major tourist attraction.

When the day came to break up the domes, campaigners sought to have them preserved as historic listed buildings. Regrettably, this plank for protection was side-stepped by government, which conveniently, so I understand, declined the opportunity on the basis that the structures were not made from the original materials, which had been replaced as part of maintenance programmes over the years.

However, if I have one regret, it is surely that I never bothered to try to get inside one of the domes. For all my familiarity with their external appearance, like most others who had ever seen them, I have absolutely no idea of what they sheltered and concealed. If only I'd thought about it in time, I'm sure it would have been possible to wangle a visit. For, recently I learned that a good friend, Sally Bucknall, actually did get inside when as Deputy National Park Officer, during a liaison visit to RAF Fylingdales, the Station Commander invited her to have a look. She vividly recounts the way the dome's innards – an enormous dish-shaped antenna - spookily moved slowly round, nudging into life like a giant science-fiction embryo preparing to hatch from its shell to wreak havoc on an unsuspecting world.

To return to Lilla Cross: who was Lilla and why did he have one named after him? The North York Moors are famed for their ancient crosses. Some were erected as way-markers, others to warn of dangerous terrain or as memorials, though the true origins of many are largely unknown, lost in the past.

Lilla was indeed a real person, a senior minister serving at the Court of King Edwin, who would become the first Christian King of Deira, and whose palace may have lain on the banks of the Derwent, possibly at Buttercrambe. In the year 626 AD, an assassin lunged at the King with a poisoned dagger. But the King was spared, when Lilla flung himself forward, absorbing a fatal blow. It is a popular though unproven belief that in honour of Lilla's sacrifice, his remains were carried up into the moors for an elaborate funeral in an existing Bronze Age burial mound, known now as Lilla Howe and that some time later a cross was placed on top.

However, English Heritage records that the design of the cross appears to date to the 10th Century – 300 years after Lilla died, and that more likely it is a boundary marker at the junction of different historic units of land.

But if we chose to think of it as a memorial to Lilla, then a memorial to Lilla it becomes, irrespective of the niceties and technicalities of its origins.

This is the world into which the infant River Derwent is born. For miles around, the landscape is blanketed by heather, mainly ling, though cross-leaved heath and bell-heather are also found. It is a place where the wind cuts sharply across the open tops and in spring the evocative calls of the curlew, golden plover, red grouse and lapwing emphasise the wildness of these hills.

In damp depressions, boggy areas are home to plants such as sundew, bog asphodel and cotton grass. And on

Top left: *The Hole of Horcum*. Top centre: *Lilla Cross*. Top right: *Fylingdales Early Warning Station – the old golf balls*.
Bottom left: *Red grouse*. Bottom centre: *Male emperor moth*. Bottom right: *Sundew*.

Top left: *Conifer trees in Langdale Forest.* Top Right: *Nuthatch.* Bottom left: *Pastoral farming in the valleys near Hackness where a lake gathered at the end of the last Ice Age.* Bottom Right: *The River Derwent in Forge Valley.*

April days, the spectacular male emperor moth, with one of the keenest senses of smell on earth, seeks out his larger and more soberly coloured mate.

Surveying this exposed and unpopulated landscape, free from the trappings of modern society, except of course for the ugly neighbour and at night the unfortunate effect on the horizon of light pollution from Tees-side and York, it is easy to be lulled into thinking that the headwaters of the Derwent and its tributaries arise in a wholly natural place. Nothing could be further from the truth. Today almost the entire land surface of Britain has been directly influenced by the actions of people, such that the only truly wild areas are found in the inter-tidal zone around the coast and sea and inland cliff faces and caves.

The open moors we see now are the product of human activity over thousands of years, from Mesolithic and Neolithic hunters, Bronze Age settlers, monastic sheep farmers and grouse moor owners. Without the present economic land use for shooting and grazing the beloved purple heather moor would, in a few years, return to woodland. I say return, for woodland is what once covered almost all of these hills.

About 100,000 years ago the climate cooled, heralding the onset of the last Ice Age in northern Britain. Before this time, the River Derwent flowed from the uplands to join the sea at Scalby, just north of Scarborough. To the south of the moors, the wide and mostly flat Vale of Pickering may at one time, have been a large inlet from the sea.

Great ice sheets advanced towards the North York Moors from the Lake District, Scotland and Scandinavia. But the ice was neither thick enough, nor powerful enough to ride over the top of the high ground. Part was deflected down the Vale of York; the rest round the northern side of the moors and down the North Sea basin. In the face of this mighty cold blast, plants and animals were forced south, though seeds may have lain locked in time in the frozen ground.

Although the ice did not cover the high ground, it did penetrate a short distance inland along the coast, up the Esk Valley to near Glaisdale and into the eastern Vale of Pickering. This would have had profound effects on the course of the River Derwent once the ice retreated.

When the thaw finally set in about 12,000 years ago, meltwater, trapped by the receding ice, the higher ground and the debris dropped on all but the southern side of the Moors, could not readily escape. A melting ice sheet means a number of things: massive amounts of material, picked up as the ice ground over the underlying rocks, is dropped where the ice stood, to form boulder clay and vast quantities of water and soil sludge go on the move. Collectively these contrived to further shape the landscape and redirect the ancient course of streams.

As the ice melted, a large lake gathered in Eskdale. When the water deepened it overtopped the hills, bursting southwards down a small pre-Ice Age valley, to gouge out Newtondale – Yorkshire's 'Grand Canyon' - in an astonishingly few decades.

A similar lake developed in the valleys around Hackness, through which the River Derwent formerly drained towards the sea. But the impacts of the ice sheet and the debris it dropped as it melted affected these too. With its historic exit blocked, the water gathered, before cutting a mini-Newtondale, now called Forge Valley, where it escaped south to the Vale of Pickering, also blocked-off from the sea.

Again, another vast lake, or possibly a series of lakes with occasional islands of higher ground formed. These too filled up until, in a repeat performance, the waters cut Kirkham Gorge as an exit to the flatlands around the head of the Humber where yet another huge lake lay.

The course of the Derwent had been redrawn. Instead of a few miles journey to the coast, it now turns inland on a circuitous, more than a hundred mile route, before its waters eventually empty through the Humber and into the North Sea.

After the ice retreated, the landscape around the

source of the Derwent saw a gradual return of plants and animals as they progressively re-colonised the bare ground. Eventually, a continuous mixed woodland of mainly oak, ash, elm, rowan and birch trees cloaked the hills, except for the very highest areas, which may have remained as open grassland.

In Mesolithic times, the first summer hunting parties visited the moors, increasing in frequency into the Neolithic period. By the Bronze age, when the climate had improved, more people lived on the hills than at any time before or since as hunter-gatherer life-styles gave way to settled farming. Trees were cleared and whether by human activity or devastating wildfires, woodland had disappeared from the tops by 1500 BC.

Catastrophically for Bronze Age communities living here, the soils were thin and poor and their fertility was soon depleted. To make matters worse, the loss of tree cover exposed the thin soils to severe erosion. In a further blow, the climate deteriorated and farming collapsed, forcing people away from the hills to which they have never returned, at least not to live. With the loss of soil quality and increased wetness, blanket peat, the forerunner of today's moorlands, began to spread.

It was to this wild landscape that monasteries were drawn, especially after the Norman Conquest. The Cistercians, who established houses at Rievaulx and Byland, were highly successful sheep farmers and introduced extensive grazing across wide areas of the hills, establishing part of the management for sheep-rearing that has endured to this day. It was not until the Victorian era, when an enthusiasm for grouse shooting developed, that the main current economic use of the land as grouse moors arose.

Not far from where the Derwent rises on Fylingdales Moor, the stream skirts the northern edge of Langdale Forest. Before the First World War the forests in this area were open land, much like the rest of the moors. But the blockade of British ports by the German navy exposed the Country's vulnerability to the loss of strategic supplies,

such as timber, for making the pit-props needed for coal mining, the main industrial driver of the time.

In 1919, the Forestry Commission was founded to tackle this deficiency. Large areas of land were needed for new plantations, so the Commission acquired it where the land was cheap, such as in the moors.

Below Langdale, the river flows towards Hackness through the area filled by the lake at the end of the Ice Age and down the sublime Forge Valley, festooned in spring with carpets of wildflowers, such as ramsons and wood anemones. These reaches are home to birds such as grey wagtails and the dipper, renowned for its ability to walk on the bed of the river in search of food, such as caddis-fly larva. These areas are also the haunt of animals such as the rare white-clawed crayfish and otter.

Where it passes through the ash woodlands, now protected as the Forge Valley and Raincliffe Woods National Nature Reserve, birdlife abounds in the trees throughout the year. Nuthatches going head-first down tree-trunks, treecreepers spiralling up, woodpeckers, jays, finches and members of the tit family can readily be seen.

At the eastern edge of Hackness village lies Hackness Hall, the family home of Lord Derwent (pronounced Darwent). As landowners, the present Lord Derwent's predecessors – the Johnstone family – in the early 19th century engaged the services of William Smith as a land agent. Though charged with matters to do with looking after the estate, Smith had another substantial string to his bow, which the family encouraged.

In his book, *The Map that Changed the World*, Simon Winchester credits Smith - or strata-Smith as he was nick-named - as the 'Father of Geology'. Further, he explores the significance of Smith's obsession with rocks and fossils and his work to advance the understanding of the way rocks were formed and laid down in sequence by single-handedly mapping the geology of Britain.

Smith's discoveries not only would have profound implications for a society still wedded to the creationist perception of the origins of species, but it also laid the foundations on which mineral and oil explorations are based today.

So important did Sir John Johnstone find Smith's work, that in 1823 he supported the construction of the Rotunda Museum in Scarborough, opened in 1828, to house displays of fossils to illustrate Smith's ideas.

When writing in 2001, Winchester lamented the down-at-heel state of this delightful building. If he should ever revisit, I think he would be encouraged by what he would see. Driven on by the uncompromising never-take-no-for-an-answer force of the present Lord Derwent, the Rotunda has been restored to celebrate again Smith's pioneering work.

After the Derwent reaches Hackness, The Sea Cut, a flood-alleviation channel, constructed at the beginning of the 19th century, drives eastwards to reunite the river with its historic outfall at the coast near Scalby, 8 miles away. The brainchild of Sir George Cayley Bt., the Cut was designed to reduce flooding in parishes at the eastern end of the Vale of Pickering, much needed in this low-lying wet and marshy place.

After the Derwent emerges from the hills, to enter its middle reaches below West Ayton, the river cuts back inland across the Vale of Pickering. But the water reaching this point down the Derwent is only a tiny proportion of the river, which passes under the Railway Street bridge in the centre of Malton. The remainder of the flow comes from a series of deep valleys etched into the uplands and spread over thirty miles below the north-south watershed of the North York Moors.

Primrose.

Overleaf: *In times of low flows, Hodge Beck is reduced to bare rock and occasional pools when the river disappears down swallow holes.*

CHAPTER TWO

Down the Valleys

Across the North York Moors, deep, southwards-facing valleys carry the Derwent's tributaries through fascinating historic landscapes, shaped by the influence of people and the elements over the years.

When William Smith published his geological map of Britain in 1815, he laid the foundations for our understanding that the rocks and the soils they produce underpin everything. They are the basis of the landscape we see and how we use it. Climate, rocks, soils and water dictate where wildlife lives, how we farm, where we build and how we choose our communications routes. Most fundamentally, rocks also determine the way the land drains.

The geology of the moors is simple. Imagine a three-tier layer cake, leaning slightly to one side and domed across the centre. The top layer (now largely worn away) comprising marine deposits, forms the flat-topped limestone Tabular Hills, running in a rising line for forty miles between Scarborough and Black Hambleton, near Osmotherley. The layer below is sandstone, laid down in an ancient river delta, where the heather now grows. Finally, the lowest layer, also of marine deposits, underlies many of the valley floors.

Over geological time these rocks have been pushed, shoved and bent by forces in the earth's crust and sliced-off by the waves when they emerged from the sea. Subsequently, small rivers cut deeply down through the rock layers and spring-sapping widened the valley sides, creating the glorious scene we enjoy today.

The upper limit of the Derwent's catchment roughly follows the line of the highest ground across Urra, Wheeldale and Fylingdales Moors. To the north and south of this line, the valleys, with their respective rivers run in a basic herringbone pattern. Those to the north drain into the River Esk and out to the North Sea at Whitby; those to the south combine forces to unite with the River Derwent.

The ideal way to appreciate the pattern and character of each of the Derwent's tributaries and their valleys is to take a journey from Forge Valley near Scarborough to Helmsley, winding across and through the Tabular Hills between the A170 road and the heather moorlands beyond.

A few miles after leaving West Ayton, the village of Brompton straddles the main road. Here, in an unexceptional building, immediately adjacent to the south side of the road and marked by a commemorative plaque, Sir George Cayley Bt., he of the imaginative Sea Cut scheme, established his workshop and most importantly, the era of manned flight was born.

Cayley was a serious genius. If Smith, just up the road, can be said to be the father of geology, Sir George was the undoubted father of aviation. Yet his achievement is barely recognised in this country. An omission, all the more unacceptable, when even the Wright Brothers, whose short flight on the plains of Kitty Hawk fifty years later is so indelibly etched in history, acknowledged their debt to Cayley and his work. Cayley's shortcoming, or was it to his credit, seemed to rest in the fact that he was more focussed on the science and experiments than public relations and adulation.

In 1853 on the slopes of Brompton Dale, north of the village, Sir George, coerced his coachman into a flying machine, known as Cayley's 'governable parachute' to make the first-ever controlled manned aircraft flight in history. On completion of the experiment, the coachman promptly resigned his post, pointing out that he had been engaged to drive horses and carriages, not to fly. A replica of his aircraft, the only one in the world to have flown, hangs in the Canadian Memorial Hanger at the Yorkshire Air Museum, not a stone's throw from the lower Derwent in Elvington. So, this little-known corner of the Derwent's catchment lies also at the base of another of the greatest influences on the modern age.

If Cayley's achievements had stopped at manned flight, he would still have rated among the all-time greats. But, to his list of sucesses must be added other major inventions: the tension-spoked wheel used in bicycles, the caterpiller-tracked vehicle, the first artificial limb and safety curtains in theatres, to name a few.

Over the centuries, Lake Pickering gradually dried up, though into the Middle Ages and even later it was still a marshy place, especially at the eastern end. With such difficult terrain for travel, roads developed along the north and south side of the Vale, rather than down the middle. The antiquity of the settlements along these roads can be readily deduced from their names. Those ending in -*ton*, -*ley*, -*ham* -*ing* and - *ingham* such as Wyke*ham*, Brompton and Thornton, Pickering and Helmsley suggest Anglian origins, from before the Norse and Danish Viking invasions of the mid-ninth Century. Others ending – *by* denote Viking origins from the 9th – 11th centuries, such as Kirkbymoorside and Aislaby. Today, these towns and villages remain united by the main A170 Thirsk to Scarborough Road. To the south, village names between Malton and Hovingham ending in -*le-street*, such as

Appleton-*le-Street* and Barton-*le-Street* record direct links with the route of a Roman road.

Standing in the middle of Pickering, a thriving tourist town, the events at this very spot at the end of the Ice Age are almost incomprehensible. This is the place where the vast torrent of water from the melting ice spewed out from Newtondale to form Lake Pickering, carrying massive quantities of gravel, ripped from the hills through which the water passed.

Today, Pickering Beck, the torrent's descendant, is a tiny affair, especially surprising when you consider the scale of the valley it drains. Newtondale, is not without good reason known as Yorkshire's 'Grand Canyon' and mercifully, in a world dominated by the motorcar, there is no road along it. Instead, one of the country's longest heritage steam railways winds its way among the wooded slopes and precipitous cliffs. Magnificent as the railway may be, it is not my favourite way to visit the valley. This, I regret to say, relies on a car journey. For sheer surprise and excitement there is no beating the approach through the villages of Lockton and Levisham.

The narrow, winding road to Levisham is quite an experience in itself, dipping and climbing through a tree-hung valley, before reaching the one-street village. Beyond Levisham, high stone-walls tightly constrain the road. Then, suddenly the ground falls away before you where a deep rift through the landscape opens up. At the bottom of another exceptionally steep hill, Levisham station, now restored as a North Eastern Railway country station of 1912, lies locked in a rural time-warp.

For those who love steam trains, this is the place to be, especially if Santa Specials are running before Christmas. When it is still and cold, billowing steam and smoke plumes hiss and thump from the locomotives to fill the crisp wintery air.

It is one of the highlights of a visit to the Moors to ride on vintage rolling-stock behind a steam locomotive. If you are really lucky it might be the elegant *Sir Nigel Gresley*, one of the timelessly-styled A4 Pacifics, or *Hartland*, a West

Top left: *A replica of Sir George Cayley Bt.'s 'Governable parachute' – the world's first manned aeroplane – in the Yorkshire Air Museum.*
Top right: *Approaching the North York Moors across the Vale of Pickering at low level and high speed in an RAF jet.* Bottom left: *Flying along Newtondale towards Levisham Station.* Bottom right: *The A4 Pacific,* Sir Nigel Gresley *pulling in to Levisham Station.*

Top left: *The calcining kilns at Roseadale Chimney Bank Top.* Top centre: *St Gregory's Minster, on the banks of Hodge Beck, Kirkdale.*
Top right: *Bilsdale seen from Newgate Bank viewing point.* Bottom left: *Rievaulx Abbey at night.*
Bottom right: *Hawnby hill and village, where extreme floods in 2005 devastated the village centre and destroyed its bridge.*

Country Class locomotive, which I can clearly recall in its real working life as it hammered, rocking and bucking, dirty and oily at the head of the Atlantic Coast Express on the mainline in Surrey where, as a boy, I used to go train-spotting with my brother.

The North Yorkshire Moors Railway, a successor to one of the earliest railways in the country, reopened in 1973 following closure under the 'Beeching Axe' in 1965. Originally constructed by George Stephenson and completed in 1836 as the Whitby to Pickering Railway, to open up trade inland with the Malton, Helmsley and Pickering areas, it utilised the valley formed by the meltwater from the ice sheets 12,000 years before.

You cannot drive down Newtondale, but you can walk or ride a horse, and of course you can take a train. There is another way to travel along this dramatic valley – fly, but few people ever have the experience.

Some years ago, as part of an educational project, I made an audiovisual presentation exploring the origins of the landscape through the eyes of a Royal Air Force jet pilot. An odd combination, you might think. But then navigating by the shape of the land and getting it right is rather important if you are to travel at low level and high speed.

On one occasion we were to trace the route of the meltwater from the ice. The pilot, Squadron Leader Ian Henley, a keen walker and North York Moors enthusiast, announced that today we would go to see the Moors Railway. He pointed out that they didn't take student pilots on this kind of sortie too early in their training. Later I would understand why.

Kitted out with flying suit, helmet and gloves we took off from RAF Linton-on-Ouse, heading towards the moors. "Descending to low level, landing light on, clear visor down," Ian directed.

As we dropped from three thousand to five hundred feet and the ground rushed past close below, a warning light on the instrument panel glowed ominously. "We have a problem, the fuel isn't feeding properly. If I tell you to eject, go and don't try to take anything with you." Ian ordered in an uncompromising voice. Some weeks earlier I had received basic ejector seat training, but like the procedures on an airliner, you don't think, or at least hope they won't be needed.

Fuel, luckily, continued to flow and the turbine-whine of the engine note, deep behind my seat, remained constant. We made a steady approach, returned to base and simply signed out another aircraft.

Flying down Newtondale at 400 miles per hour, tracing the bends in the valley, is undoubtedly the most exhilarating thing I have ever experienced, one from which I have never fully come down to earth. There, below the nose and almost within touching distance ran the railway, the cliffs of the gorge beside us, and in steep tight turns the ranks of conifers crowding in at our shoulder. In barely a minute or two we were over Newbridge, now Pickering below and then we burst, like the meltwater out across the wide Vale.

Heading back to Linton-on-Ouse, we made a detour to my house. Pulling tightly round Butterwick, alongside the River Rye, I was to see my breakfast for the second time that day, immediately above where I saw it for the first time, thus completely contradicting the laws of gravity.

If Newtondale is home to some of the most dramatic natural events in recent geological time, then Rosedale, down which flows the River Seven, takes the crown for human-induced change. From the top of Rosedale Chimney Bank, the summit of one of the steepest roads in the Country, the view embraces an apparently unaltered rural scene. Yet, unbelievably, one hundred and fifty years ago this valley was home to iron mining activity on a substantial industrial scale.

Mines penetrated the hillsides at several locations. And calcining kilns, used to reduce the weight of the iron ore, on both east and west sides were linked by a railway running round the head of the Dale, almost to the watershed by Ralph Cross and the highest point of the moors. At Blakey junction, close to the Lion Inn pub on Blakey Ridge the track headed across the open moor to near Ingleby

Greenhow. Here wagons were lowered by steel ropes down a steep incline, too steep to be negotiated by locomotives. From the foot of the incline, the ore could then be transported to the blast furnaces on the rivers Wear and Tees.

At Blakey Junction, where the railway ran under the road, part of the bridge parapet and cutting, together with the route of the track-bed can still be seen. On this high ridge, only a short distance separates Rosedale from Farndale. Walk a hundred yards and soon the road descends steeply and another fine view opens up.

At the end of the 1960s and into early 1970s proposals to construct a reservoir, drowning the the landscape of Upper Farndale, were met with dismay. Eventually, the scheme was rejected by Parliament, to be replaced by the Barmby Barrage at the mouth of the Derwent, which would prevent the tidal water of the Ouse from flowing upstream so that the river could be used for drinking water supply.

Farndale is widely known for its drifts of wild daffodils peppering the banks of the River Dove in spring. Smaller and more delicate than cultivated varieties, the flowers exert a magnetic influence on thousands of visitors who arrive on foot and by car and coach each year.

About a mile west of Kirkbymoorside, the present A170 road swings south before rejoining the line of the ancient route. But the old road still exists, dipping to cross a ford in a tight valley where the Hodge Beck drains from Bransdale.

Centred round the beck lie three fascinating places, one of which in the early 19th Century would rewrite the story of the British landscape. As a child I was keen on rivers. I can clearly recall thumbing the pages of books about the way they behaved – meanders, ox-bow lakes, erosion on the outside of bends, deposition on the inside … and the mysterious one, swallow holes, where a river would simply disappear underground to emerge elsewhere, or perhaps never to be seen again. What a fascinating idea, a place where you could put coloured dye and then look for it appearing somewhere else.

Come to Kirkdale in winter and a full-bodied stream boils over the ford; return in mid-summer and chances are the riverbed will be dry, or reduced to a series of isolated pools. Upstream, the intriguing river has disappeared underground.

To the north east of the ford, regenerating woodland obscures an old quarry. Its small scale belies the enormity of the revelations made here almost two centuries ago. In 1821, as workmen quarried away the face, they discovered a mysterious cave. Inside lay a jumble of animals' bones and teeth. Dismissing them as the remains of cattle, the workmen threw large quantities into the river. Others were carried away among quarried road stone.

By chance, a local Doctor, John Harrison, noticed the unusual fragments lying on a roadway. Tracing their source back to Kirkdale, a specialist, Dr Buckland, called in from Oxford, made an astonishing discovery. The bones and teeth belonged to an extraordinary range of wild animals, some extinct and many no longer seen in Britain, including straight-tusked elephant, hippopotamus, giant deer, bison, rhinoceros, wolf, brown bear and large numbers of hyenas. The remains fell into two distinct groups. Some were from a cold climate, while others originated from hotter places. Mixed with the remains lay hundreds of encrusted hyena droppings.

Piecing the jigsaw puzzle together suggested that the cave had been a hyena's den before the last Ice Age more than 100,000 years ago. Much more than that, the range of species proved that Britain had at one time been a sub-tropical place and at another extreme a cold, dry steppe environment.

Much was deduced from the discovery in this quiet corner, beside Hodge Beck. But a fundamental puzzle remained. Everything in the cave was covered in a thick layer of mud. At the time this was attributed to the biblical flood – no one then knew about the Ice Age, or Lake Pickering, the rising waters of which had drowned the entrance and covered the remains.

Today, little survives of the cave – merely a narrow slit

about a metre high. But it isn't too hard to imagine hyenas standing in its entrance at night surrounded by the sounds associated with the African Plains.

In the days when I worked in a publisher's office we organised a Christmas outing to Kirkbymoorside. On the way back we decided to sneak into Kirkdale Cave. At the time, I didn't realise it lay on private land. Spotting the cave entrance during the day is easy, but shinning up the old quarry face in the wet and pulling yourself into the entrance proved more of a challenge at night. Inside the cave the roof is low, the space confined and claustrophobic. We switched off our torch and sat quietly. It was cold, dark and a bit scary. Someone suggested that there was no limit to what you might hear and see if you concentrated hard enough, as you shared a place with those animals from down the avenues of time, especially when you'd spent a while in the pub beforehand.

Tucked among the trees on the opposite bank to the quarry, St Gregory's Minster, with its Saxon origins is an idyllic spot. Its setting in this narrow wooded valley is the stuff of our romantic image of England.

In 1771, under the porch on the church's south wall, just above the doorway, the most complete Saxon sundial in the world was discovered. An obvious question for the first-time visitor is, what earthly use is a sundial hidden away undercover in the shade? But the porch, a much later addition, was not there when the sundial was installed. Helpfully, an inscription on its face enables accurate dating to within a few years before the Norman Conquest.

'Orm, Gamel's son bought St Gregory's minster when it was all ruined and fallen down, and he caused it to be built new from the ground in the days of Edward and in the days of Tosti the earl' it records, then finishes with a delightful expression:

'This is the day's sun marker at each hour. Haworth made me and Brand, priests.'

Mention of Tostig, King Harold's brother, who was Earl of Northumberland in 1055 and banished in 1065, narrows to a mere 10 years the time when the priests would have cut their stone block, carving the dial and its message to inform generations of churchgoers of the passing hours.

Beyond Helmsley, a pantile and stone village, beloved of tourists and large groups of motorcyclists on a Sunday, the Teesside road climbs up into the limestone hills towards Bilsdale, sweeping through the undulating landscape.

At the top of the long haul out of Helmsley, Newgate Bank, a Forestry Commission viewpoint affords a wide vista over Bilsdale where the River Seph takes over drainage of the hills. On the moor top opposite, the slender structure of Bilsdale TV transmitter mast, hosts one of the tallest lifts in Europe. Below it, in late summer, the steep hillsides assume the appearance of a breathtaking multi-coloured tapestry, with purple heather, shading into the reds and green of bilberry and in places the orange and brown of bracken. Sometimes the weather conditions contrive to unite summer and autumn colours in a combined display.

Bilsdale also lays claim to another spectacle, the Bilsdale Cricket Club's steeply sloping pitch. Sitting behind the New Sun Inn on a summer's evening - the Old Sun Inn, a thatched stone house known as Spout House and one of the oldest buildings in the National Park is on the other side of the car park - a pint of beer in hand, while marvelling at the additional pace of a downhill stroke, contributes to the sheer eccentricity of it all.

To the west of the viewpoint, at the bottom of Bilsdale, the River Seph joins the River Rye. Close to the Rye, in Rievaulx village, a small group of houses, some thatched, conform to a Christmas card image of our mellow countryside of the past. In this frost hollow on a winter's day, a temperature inversion will hold a layer of sweet-smelling wood smoke across the rooftops, drifting into the fading evening light.

After the Norman Conquest in 1066, these moors, as elsewhere in remote England saw a resurgence in monasticism. The monks took full advantage of their isolated locations to establish a way of life separate from the pressures of the world. Rievaulx Abbey, set below its wooded hillside is unconventional for a religious building. Instead of being built on a customary east-west axis, because of limited space alongside the River Rye, it was aligned north-south, though the relationship between chancel and nave, north and south transepts and other structures was maintained.

Some years ago, while making an audio-visual presentation about the monasteries of the North York Moors, I decided that it would be interesting to photograph the abbey at night. After a bit of a struggle with English Heritage, who have 'rules' and paperwork for this sort of thing, they agreed that I could just go and do it. I thought that if I took a treble recorder and tape recorder with me I could create the soundtrack, believing that it would gain something from being played within the echoing shapes of the soaring ruins.

At ten o'clock, my companion, Jan and I clambered carefully and quietly over the back entrance gate. The moon was full. Thick mist swirled in and out fading the eerie light, then brightening it up like a natural dimmer-switch.

In the centre of the nave the vast pillars towered in black silhouettes above us. Between the arches bright light from the moon repeated the shapes across the abbey floor. There was no colour, just moonlight. Beyond the precincts the slight grumbling sound of the river could be heard.

I took my photographs, picked up the recorder, switched on the tape and started self-consciously to play the 1960s Yardbirds haunting song 'Still I'm Sad'. 'See the wind come softly blowing time into my heart' run some of the words. It suited the atmosphere of the place.

What happened next could not have been predicted. In response to my first few notes, hundreds of pigeons and doves, which had been silently roosting in the ruins, started to coo in unison, on and on in response to my playing. If I stopped, they stopped. When I started again, the birds started too. It was very gentle, nothing sinister, nothing threatening, just very moving and powerful. It wasn't

frightening among the ruins; more a feeling of being suspended in a strange unrepeatable point in time.

We headed back towards the gate. Looking over our shoulders to where the nave had been silhouetted by the moonlight, the mist had closed in, the moon had disappeared and the buildings had vanished into the pitch dark of the night.

Below Rievaulx, the River Rye passes under a 200 years old stone bridge. Before the road down from Sutton bank via Sproxton was constructed, this was the main road from Thirsk to Scarborough. Here, in summer, the air by Rievaulx Bridge is perfumed with the strong smell of aniseed, from the sweet cicely flowers which cloak the banks.

Downstream, the Rye cuts through the Duncombe Park Estate, the home of Lord Feversham. Throughout the countryside ancient trees have largely been removed. But Duncombe Park is different. In its delightful grounds you will still find a fine array of Veteran trees as they are now known, including the tallest lime tree in the country at just over 144 feet tall. Such continuity and longevity is critical for wildlife and the woodlands are renowned for their variety of insects, which live on mature trees and decaying timber, and are deservedly recognised as a National Nature Reserve.

Leaving the parklands of Duncombe Park, the River Rye runs close to Helmsley Castle, a massive stone structure managed now by English Heritage, before flowing under Helmsley Bridge.

On the 19th June 2005, the world changed forever for Hawnby, a village upstream, when the awesome power of erratic weather exerted itself on the tight valleys leading to Helmsley, dropping a month's rainfall in just three hours and sending a wall of water and mud crashing down through the village, wrecking its centre and smashing away its bridge before thundering on to take chunks out of Helmsley Bridge as well. What happens further downstream in the middle and lower reaches, after the rivers and streams of the Derwent's upper catchment combine forces, also regularly makes headline news.

Above: *Helmsley Castle.* **Overleaf:** *Once a lakeland 12000 years ago, the Vale of Pickering with its fine lake-bed soils is a premier cereal producing area.*

CHAPTER THREE
Through the Middle Reaches

From the Vale of Pickering the River Derwent splits the twin towns of Malton and Norton before flowing into Kirkham Gorge and on to Stamford Bridge, where King Harold beat the invading Norwegians in 1066.

Occasionally when the air is still, a layer of low-lying mist will fill the whole of the Vale of Pickering. At such moments it is as if the ancient lake lies before you.

Whether it was a single stretch of water, a series of lakes, or a lake with a number of islands is a matter of debate, though if the water had been deep enough, at least to start with, it could have been a continuous sheet, greater in extent than any existing lake in England today.

The Derwent is regarded as having the best example of a classic river profile in the country – upper, middle and lower reaches – with its wildlife species virtually intact.

They can be broadly categorised as the stretches where the river and its tributaries run swiftly (upper), then slow down (middle), until the influence of the sea backs it up to force the river in times of flood out of its banks onto the surrounding land (lower).

For my purposes, the start of the middle reaches can be conveniently defined as the points where the river and its tributaries run under the bridges on the main A170 Thirsk to Scarborough road, down to where the first signs of the floodplain appear about half way between Stamford Bridge and Sutton upon Derwent.

At school, our Geography teacher Percy Silley made much of the agricultural quality of the Vale of Pickering.

School was in Kingston upon Thames, far away from north-east Yorkshire. I had no idea what it might be like, but its significance for farming, emphasised by Percy, stuck in my mind, even though I'd never been there.

Few major settlements have been established in the middle of the Vale, no doubt because of its low-lying and waterlogged conditions before the days of drainage for agriculture. Instead, most have been built on the surrounding slopes, just above the historically wetter ground.

Until the railways' economic slide in the face of the inexorable advance of the motor vehicle and improvement in road conditions, the railway network echoed the fringe-pattern of settlement. A tile map on a wall in York Railway station shows the extensive network of the North Eastern Railway in 1923, preserving in glazed ceramics the ghosts of stations such as Gilling East, Amotherby and Barton-le-Street.

As well as the rail-routes around the Vale, main line connections linked York, Malton and Scarborough (1845) and also Malton with Pickering (1848); the latter line, uniting the previously isolated Whitby to Pickering railway with the rest of the national network.

To reach Malton, the Scarborough line utilised Kirkham Gorge, running tightly alongside the river Derwent between the Yorkshire Wolds and the Howardian

Hills, just as the Whitby to Pickering railway followed the meltwater channel down Newtondale a decade before. And also like Newtondale, there is no road.

Once clear of the hills at West Ayton, below the stone bridge, constructed from stone cannibalised from the ruins of Ayton Castle, the Derwent runs through only one settlement, Yedingham, before reaching Malton fifteen or so miles downstream. In 1702, an Act of Parliament provided for making the river navigable from its mouth up to Yedingham, and then on, with the aid of a new cut to Scarborough Mills.

The enabling Act, envisaged a statutory navigation run in two sections, from the mouth of the Derwent to Malton and thence from Malton to Scarborough. Although this was the clear intention, no one seems to know exactly where Scarborough Mills lay, although, I did once see a single pencil sketch in an obscure archive showing a location somewhere to the west of the town, which sadly I failed to record.

In the event, the navigation to Malton was completed about 1720, but it was almost a hundred years later in 1814 before it was extended to Yedingham, though it never did reach Scarborough, its original destination.

The extension to Yedingham was an economically shaky affair. Within thirty years its day was done and the dams at New and Old Malton, which held the river at levels suitable for milling and navigation, were removed in the interests of land drainage.

Careful study of an Ordnance Survey map of the central Vale of Pickering shows that the river is not as it was in the past. Where formerly it meandered along a winding route, often its course runs unnaturally straight.

These artificial changes to its course are most obvious where, like many rivers, it formed an administrative boundary. Hence, in places, dotted lines delineating Parish limits, which in the past followed the mid-stream point of the river, now chart an arbitrary and wandering route over dry land, evidence of the hands of drainage engineers straightening its course over the years.

From the other end of the valley at Helmsley Bridge in the west, the River Rye collects up the flow of a number of the rivers we crossed on our journey along the south of the Moors, until it joins the Derwent at Rye Mouth, a few miles above Malton. If flow quantity is anything to go by, the main river below this point should never have been called the Derwent, but, more appropriately, the River Rye, which contributes most of the water below Rye Mouth.

The Rye only passes through a few more settlements across the Vale of Pickering than the Derwent. Nunnington, the historic home at Nunnington Hall of Clive of India, is first. It then skirts West and East Ness, where the springs deliver up the most fabulous drinking water from the aquifer, charged by the surrounding hills.

Further downstream, Butterwick, a tiny village of seven houses and a church, where I lived and worked for twenty-five years stands on its banks.

Since it was built in the mid-1800s, Butterwick Bridge and its river have formed a focal point for village life. The river is also a magnet for wildlife, with herons, kingfishers, swans, ducks, grey wagtails, and passage migrants such as sandpipers.

Alongside the bridge, Henry Leeson, a local farmer, made a village seat from an elm tree killed by Dutch Elm Disease. Each year we would celebrate the seat at midsummer, toasting it and the changing year at the moment the setting sun touched the horizon above Helmsley. Well that was the intention, but on most occasions, it would either be raining or dull and the sun nowhere to be seen.

From Henry's seat, you could look straight down into a bend in the river or far up into the moors on the northern skyline, at the very top of the watershed from where much of the water in the river systems had come.

It was quite uncanny to lean on Butterwick bridge parapets, for here, people of the past who had similarly whiled away the hours are permanently remembered. Carved into the bridge coping stones are outlines of hands, initials and little messages engraved by children and

Top left: *Carvings in the coping stones of Butterwick bridge record idle moments of villagers in the past.* Top right: *The River Rye below Butterwick village.* Bottom left: An aerial view of *the River Derwent running alongside the railway between the twin towns of Malton and Norton.* Bottom right: *A tile map in York station depicts the North Eastern Railway's network in 1923.*

Left: *Kirkham Gorge was cut by meltwater escaping from the Vale of Pickering at the end of the Ice Age.*
Top right: *The ruins of the 12th Century Kirkham Abbey.* Bottom right: *A Victorian watercolour painting of a train passing through Kirkham Gorge in the early days of the York to Scarborough Railway*

lovers. On a frosty morning when the coping stones are covered with rime and the sun is low, these small reminders stand clear in the frost, their authors still present, above the flash of the kingfisher and the swirling water in their marks made long ago.

It was on the bridge that I first met Sydney, that's 'Sydney with a 'y' Jameson', as he would announce himself, who would contribute to a strand of the campaigns to safeguard the rivers. Sydney, who was in his 80s, deserves to be remembered as a 'stepping stone' who through his newpaper articles would nudge the direction of the future's flow.

Living in Butterwick gave an early warning of flood conditions to come for the rest of the Derwent system downstream. Whatever happened here would be repeated about twelve hours later in Malton and a day or two after that in the floodplain of the Lower Derwent Valley.

One of the oft-quoted statements about the Derwent was penned by Henry VIII's chronicler Leland on a visitation to Wressle in the Lower Derwent in 1520: 'this river at great rains rageth and overfloweth, much of the ground thereabouts being low meadows'.

At times of very heavy rains in 1998 and 2000 some of the biggest floods in recent history turned large parts of the Vale of Pickering, the centre of Malton and Norton and the Lower Derwent Valley, into vast sheets of water, greater than anyone could remember happening before. Imagine the amount of water involved. This was not a lake, but a head of flowing water continuously passing through.

But there was a local upside to being cut off for nearly a fortnight. We were able to measure and trace the absolute levels reached before the river Rye burst its banks and drained away from the village. The water came within two feet of the houses, but three feet below their level. While Butterwick survived unscathed, Malton and Norton were not anywhere near as lucky. At the bridge between the twin towns, floods swamped many homes, and the sight of boating in the road through the persisting water made headline news, flashed around the world.

Floods had been into people's houses here many times over the years. Maybe the difference now is that in the days before electricity, electrical appliances and fitted carpets people would have just lifted their belongings, let the water in and out and carried on. It would be much more difficult to do that today.

Below Rye Mouth the Rye becomes the Derwent. This is where its specially protected wildlife sites begin in earnest. From here to its mouth, except for a section though the centre of Malton, which has still to be notified, the River is designated a Special Area of Conservation under the Habitats Regulations. These derive their power from Europe-wide legislation, the European Union Habitats Directive, which protects our finest natural areas.

Before reaching Malton, the Derwent skirts Old Malton, a distinct settlement about a mile north of the main town. Paradoxically, 'New' Malton is older than 'Old' Malton, having been a small town in Roman times, before being replaced by the Roman Garrison of Derventio in about AD80.

In Old Malton, alongside the river, lies an open grassy area, where, before the recent raising of the flood banks, you could still trace depressions in the banks at the site of a cut and lock, which carried the statutory navigation to Yedingham past the mill dam.

Nearby, St Mary's Church, a remnant of the mediaeval Gilbertine Priory built between 1154 and 1174, is still in use.

High on the tower a square owl box, built into the original stonework, provides a nesting place for barn owls, a useful biological control of vermin in the monastic precincts of yore.

Upstream from Malton road bridge, another mill dam straddled the river. Although some of the buildings still stand, the dam which retained the head of water to work the mill, like its counterpart at Old Malton was removed in the 1840s to help land drainage.

Immediately opposite the site of Malton Mill, a series of islands stood in the river. Originally, in 1845, the newly constructed York and Scarborough Railway traversed this 'archipelago' on a wooden viaduct, but by the early 20th Century the gaps had been filled in to make a continuous bed for the track.

Between the riverbank and the track, construction of the railway isolated some small sections of gardens, which belonged to properties in Commercial Street, Norton. Until 2004, one hundred and sixty years later, one of these parcels survived, still with its variety of fruit trees, before being obliterated by the engineering works connected with new defences erected in response to the recent floods.

During the highest floods, the platform at Malton Station, close to the River, stood not beside a railway line but a long stretch of water as far as you could see in either direction. The submerged line and damaged signalling and other control systems, rendered the trains out of action for weeks, while buses replaced them on journeys to Scarborough and York.

Derventio, as Malton was known in Roman times, lay at a river crossing on the road linking over the Yorkshire Wolds from the Humber and on to the north. Roman Potteries were established downstream at Crambe Beck and at Menethorpe another road dropped down from the Wolds, possibly to a river crossing and on up into the Howardian Hills.

Today, Malton, an attractive market town and celebrated rural shopping centre, is mostly noted for its horse racing connections, curiously without a racecourse, and, as a recent epicentre for news of floods. Undoubtedly, the leading candidate for its most famous personality in history, must surely be Edmund Burke, the local MP between 1781 and 1794. For among many of his other profound sayings connected with freedom, it was he who coined 'all that is necessary for the triumph of evil is that good men do nothing'.

In the heyday of the railways, south of Malton, trains to York stopped at long-gone halts, Huttons Ambo, Castle Howard and Kirkham Abbey, where the line wound through Kirkham Gorge.

During construction of the railway some re-engineering of the river's course was needed. Rather than build two bridges and gradients at Welham to twice clear vessels using the river on a large U-bend, nature was given a helping hand and a short-cut cut across the top of the 'U' left an isolated loop, which still holds water today.

Travelling by train through Kirkham Gorge at any time of the year is to glimpse into the secret world of the river, a bit like looking at it from a mobile hide as the train follows the historic escape route for water from the Vale of Pickering. No bankside development, just waterside reeds, wet woodland, boggy farmland grazed by cattle and, on emerging from the gorge, on the opposite side of the river, the impressive ruins of 13th Century Kirkham Priory.

Below Kirkham, Howsham Wood slopes steeply to the water's edge, before the train turns away from the river through Barton-Hill, another former stop, and on to the grand Victorian station, the largest in the world when opened in 1877, at York.

The river heads past Howsham and its solid early 17th Century Hall, over Howsham weir, where the gothic-style old mill building is being restored, to Buttercrambe with its imposing Queen Anne House of 1725, and the possible site of King Edwin's 7th Century palace.

Buttercrambe Mill, now converted to a private dwelling, has a special claim to fame. All thoroughbred racehorses are descended from three animals. One, the Darley Arabian, with which it is said 95% of modern throughbred stock are linked, was stabled in the building beside the mill around 1710.

Within Aldby Park, the Darley family estate, a gauging weir constructed across the river, records flows as part of the management of the lower river for water abstraction and supply at Loftsome Bridge.

At Stamford Bridge a three-span stone bridge, built in 1727, carries the York to Bridlington road. To the south a redundant railway viaduct, once the bearer of the York to Beverley railway line, is silhouetted against the light. When the river was threatened with development for marinas, renowned local naturalist and highly amusing broadcaster, Michael Clegg, who lived in Stamford Bridge at the time, caught someone pushing bits of the viaduct into the water.

When challenged, the offender explained indignantly that he was 'doing his bit for conservation' by pushing brickwork into the river to stop boats. "But the viaduct is an historic building and we want to protect that too", Mike pointed out.

After the Battle of Fulford and immediately before the Battle of Hastings in 1066, King Harold (Harold Godwinson, the English King) engaged King Harald Hardrada of Norway in the Battle of Stamford Bridge, thought to have taken place to the south of the present village, straddling the Low Catton road.

There was once a tradition in the area of making meat pies in the shape of a swine tub, to celebrate the tale of events surrounding the Norwegian soldier, who, standing on the bridge over the river single-handedly held up Harold's advance.

To deal with the problem, an English soldier found a swine tub (used for scalding hair off pigs), there being no boats on the river here, got in it and floated unnoticed down under the wooden bridge. Below the bridge, he thrust a sword upwards through a gap in the planks, despatching the soldier and freeing the way with one eye-watering lunge, so the story goes.

No one knows where the site of that bridge lay, but it must have been a narrow one, if a single soldier could defend it. Perhaps it might have been at the site of the predecessor to the present bridge. This spanned the river a few hundred yards upstream at the outer edge of the mill pool immediately opposite the road leading to Low Catton.

Before Sutton Mill dam was built, the tidal effects on the Derwent probably ran to a point somewhere between Sutton upon Derwent and Stamford Bridge. But for all practical purposes throughout recorded history, Sutton dam was the limit of the tide until the Barmby Tidal Barrage was commissioned and obstructed its natural flows in 1977.

As sea levels began to rise when the ice sheets retreated and the land tilted slowly upwards, relieved by the removal of the weight of ice, so the Derwent's floodplain developed in response to the levels of the sea. At times of high flow, the swollen river would spread out of its banks, depositing silt and building up the surrounding land.

The floodplain of the Lower Derwent is the river's greatest natural asset. From the air, at times of high flood levels, the whole shimmering sheet of water forms a huge lake, twelve miles long by up to almost a mile wide in places. Its first traces are found at Kexby Bridge along Low Catton Ings and Newton Mask, but it is below the Escrick Moraine a mile south of Sutton that the full effect emerges. Here, the influence of the river expands to embrace thousands of acres of meadow and marsh. And the designations of legal protections for wildlife expand with it.

The Lower Derwent Valley, including parts of the old Pocklington Canal and its adjacent meadows and pastures enjoys a catalogue of protection as a Site of Special Scientific Interest (SSSI), Ramsar Wetland of International Importance, European Union Special Protection Area for Birds (SPA) and a European Union Special Area of Conservation (SAC), while substantial areas are also designated a National Nature Reserve (NNR). (See map p47)

But this is not a landscape set apart for wildlife. Its beautiful meadows full of wildflowers would not survive without farmers. This is a living, working example of nature conservation almost wholly bedded into farming and a leading example of how the relationship between the world of conservation and that of economic agriculture can achieve a very important goal.

Overleaf: *At low temperatures, the flooded Lower Derwent Valley can turn to a continuous twelve-mile long sheet of ice.*

CHAPTER FOUR

Across the Floodplain

Spectacular flood-meadows full of wildlife echo a traditional agricultural landscape of the past on a scale rarely seen in Britain today.

One morning in early 1980, I awoke with an idea which would eventually lead me to a unique involvement with the River Derwent and particularly the riverside fields known as the Ings – an old Norse word for seasonally flooded low-lying meadows – stretching between Sutton and South Duffield near the river's mouth

I had a notion it would be good to buy a piece of land for nature conservation. Trouble was, at the same time we needed a new car. It was a hard decision, but in the end we settled on the land. A car would rust away, but the right sort of land and its wildlife, if looked after properly would renew itself each year.

I called Stephen Warburton, who suggested that Sarah Priest, a conservation officer with the then Nature Conservancy Council, would be the person to ask for advice. By coincidence, that very morning, Sarah had learned of a Derwent hay meadow belonging to an elderly lady who had died, which would be coming up for sale. She made the link to the sellers for me and a purchase was soon agreed.

Rather irresponsibly, I suppose, Jan and I never saw the land before we decided to buy it. I had simply asked Sarah: "Is this place important for wildlife?", and took the decision on the strength of her response.

"Of the highest order and it has no legal protection", she explained. "And the flowers are wonderful."

Owning the meadow soon brought into sharp focus the realities of managing land for farming and wildlife. A licensee has to be found to take the crop; grips (small drainage channels) have to be cleared; ragwort, which, in hay is poisonous to animals, has to be pulled and in due course when it was notified as a Site of Special Scientific Interest and a collection of other designations were applied to the land, regulations had to be observed; all experiences which nevertheless would stand me in good stead in the future.

Late on a summer's evening we made our first visit down the dirt track, to where the floodplain of the Derwent dramatically widens. Pausing at the top of the slope on the Escrick Moraine, in the exact place where the ice sheet that covered northern Britain met Lake Humber, the meadow landscape stretched into the distance beyond Wheldrake Ings.

A mile away, a solitary bell chimed out across the still meadows from Thicket priory, home to a closed order of Carmelite nuns. Out of the tower a barn owl drifted down, its ghostly shape jinking, moth-like and low over the vegetation, quartering in search of its prey.

From where we stood, the ice front would have

stretched round as far Barnsley in the western side of Yorkshire and to Wroot beyond Doncaster in the south; behind us would have been a frozen world all the way to the North Pole.

Hemmed in by a combination of debris from the ice sheet and higher ground in north Nottinghamshire and north Lincolnshire, the waters of Lake Humber gathered. As in the Vale of Pickering no one is sure whether it was a single expanse of water, or a series of smaller lakes. Either way, when it drained it gave rise to the flatlands now known as the Humberhead Levels.

It was difficult to make out exactly which piece of land we had bought, for the Ings are generally strip-farmed without hedges and fences, or any obvious marks on the ground; only territorial memory indicates to the owners where they believe one strip ends and another begins.

Naively I arranged for marker posts to be put in. Calculating their positions from the purchase map and the area described in the deeds, then relating that to a feature-less expanse of grass was not easy.

Not a day had passed before William Ward, the adjacent farmer was on the phone; the positions of the posts were wrong. Tactfully he pointed out the error and while not exactly the best start for non-farmers, it did mean we had met our neighbour, with whom we have remained good friends ever since.

The Derwent Ings, stretching for more than 2000 acres, is a working landscape of great antiquity. Possibly farmed in a similar way since before the Norman Conquest, each year a single hay cut is taken, followed by grazing of the re-growth – the aftermath - with sheep or cattle. The Ings are also a landscape of wide seasonal contrasts; in spring-time a sea of wildflowers, in winter a wild, damp and lonely home to thousands of wildfowl and wading birds such as swans and geese, many from Iceland, Greenland and northern Russia.

With so many birds, wildfowling provided an important source of food in the past. For some it was a job.

Working silently down the drainage channels in pursuit of his quarry, the legendary Snowden Slights, is remembered as the punt-gunner, who bagged 75 lapwing with a single blast of shot from his largest gun on one occasion and 45 mallard and wigeon on another. Slights' punt and guns, now powerfully displayed in the Yorkshire Museum in York, offer a poignant reminder of an era and way of life, which has slipped away. But fundamentals of his time endure in this little-changed place; the smells of new-mown hay at harvest time, mud and wetness and the sounds of the wind and wildfowl out on the flood are exactly the same.

For most of its journey through the Ings the Derwent lies tucked down between deep banks, often out of sight from the surrounding roads and settlements, built well back from the river to avoid the floods. But in a few places the view is clear; from the entrance to Yorkshire Wildlife Trust's Wheldrake Ings Nature Reserve; from the main road at Bubwith , Breighton and Loftsome Bridge, and from outside the Ferryboat Inn in West Cottingwith. And even when the river rises in times of flood its outline frequently becomes lost in an overwhelmingly wide expanse of water.

Until the mid 20th Century two historic wooden drawbridges spanned the river into Wheldrake Ings. Both have now been demolished, one being replaced by a Bailey bridge, with the help of the army and the other removed entirely.

It was in the vicinity of East Cottingwith, just south of Wheldrake Ings, that the last recorded specimen of the Burbot, is reputed to have been caught in Britain. Thought by many to be extinct, but only 'gone missing for a bit' to we optimists, if a live Burbot still survives anywhere in the United kingdom, it would be nice to think that it might be in the Derwent.

A fish caught in Elvington did survive in a glass case in The City Arms in Fishergate York, the base at the time for the York Amalgamation of Anglers, until it was stolen from the wall one night in 1989. In 2005 'The case of the missing

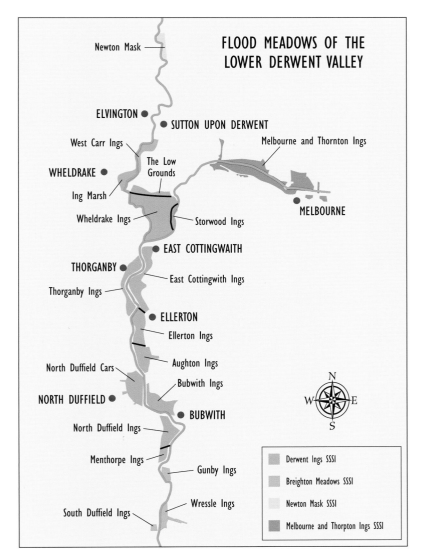

FLOOD MEADOWS OF THE
LOWER DERWENT VALLEY

Newton Mask

ELVINGTON
SUTTON UPON DERWENT
West Carr Ings
Melbourne and Thornton Ings
The Low
Grounds
WHELDRAKE
Ing Marsh
Wheldrake Ings
Storwood Ings
MELBOURNE
EAST COTTINGWAITH
THORGANBY
East Cottingwith Ings
Thorganby Ings
ELLERTON
Ellerton Ings
North Duffield Cars
Aughton Ings
Bubwith Ings
NORTH DUFFIELD
BUBWITH
North Duffield Ings
Menthorpe Ings
Gunby Ings
Wressle Ings
South Duffield Ings

Derwent Ings SSSI
Breighton Meadows SSSI
Newton Mask SSSI
Melbourne and Thorpton Ings SSSI

Left: *A map of the Lower Derwent Valley shows the settlements and the specially protected areas for nature conservation.*
A mosaic of landholdings forms the Lower Derwent Valley National Nature Reserve. Top Right: *Small machinery producing rectangular bales twenty years ago has been superseded by larger equipment.* Bottom right: *Modern and heavier equipment produces round bales.*

Top left: *Looking south from above Sutton upon Derwent, a vast flood reveals the full extent of the Lower Derwent floodplain.*
Top right: *Ellerton Church sits dramatically in its landscape.* Bottom left: *The Elvington Burbot, caught by F. Sollitt 1924, stolen by ??? 1989.*
Bottom right: *Whooper swan.*

Burbot' featured in an eccentric New Year's Eve Radio 4 programme presented by Chris Yates, when research uncovered that: York police confirm that the file is still open; many years ago a local farming character caught and ate one; and how a member of York Amalgamation of Anglers 'was gutted' when the specimen in the glass case was pinched. And on the subject of the last revelation, I know they would rather like it back.

While physical changes to the landscape at the end of the Ice Age were on a massive continent-wide scale, those affecting the river more recently are modest. Several hundred years ago the Derwent's course altered or was deliberately changed just below the Escrick Moraine. Originally it curved westwards around an area known as Bank Island at Wheldrake, then turned sharply east along the foot of the slope, before heading south to a point between East and West Cottingwith, opposite the Ferryboat Inn. Elsewhere, a number of sharp bends were straightened during the 20th Century. And in early times, perhaps during the Roman era, the mouth was re-aligned westwards.

On a map of 1615, produced for the Duke of Bolton (oft though very erroneously know as the Mad Duke of Bolton according to Drake in his *History and Antiquities of York* 1735) the route of a proposed canal ran from the Humber, near the confluence with the River Trent, directly to York. Near where it crossed the Derwent both old and new courses are shown, surrounding two distinct islands at Wheldrake Ings and Bank Island.

It seems certain that the Roman settlement at Storwood, excavated by the University of Hull as part of the Humber Wetlands Project, was established close to the banks of the old course, no doubt utilising the tidal river as a communications route to towns on other rivers and to the sea. Although nothing of the settlement is now visible, a plan of the evidence of a road, houses and gardens lying a few inches below the surface of the fields was mapped as part of the archaeological research.

Although it is not clear exactly when the river's course changed at Wheldrake, the old course, known locally as the Darren, is still visible as a wet depression and drainage channel across the Ings.

As in the Vale of Pickering, confirmation that this change happened in relatively recent history is shown by the administrative boundaries. In Wheldrake Ings and at Bank Island, the boundary between North Yorkshire (The old North Riding) and the East Riding follows the old course to both east and west of the river's present line.

Each visit to the Ings brings a new seasonal experience – the nesting birds, the rare flowers, the staggering sunsets, the chill of a winter's morning, or a huge harvest moon rising over the empty space. Nothing quite compares however, with the scene if the flooded Ings freeze.

When a flood freezes here strange things happen. As it subsides and water drains out from underneath, the ice drops onto the undulations of the land below, resulting in gentle 'hills' where the ice has bent over the contours of the land, but because of its thickness, does not break. Early January 1982 was exceptionally cold for many days. Temperatures dipped to −14°C and an extensive flood throughout the Ings turned to one continuous sheet of ice.

Above the ice, freezing fog obscured the distant view and millions of frost-flower ice crystals grew at regular intervals, every few inches, like decorations purposely placed by an unseen hand for miles across the surface.

Standing on the ice produced a dramatic effect. The additional weight of a person proved too much. With each step the ice would crack, sending a sound similar to a fishing line ripping through water, a sort of zizizizizizi… zipping when the crack accelerated hundreds of yards into the distance and out of earshot, as the pent-up tension in the bent ice released.

Until the Barmby Tidal Barrage was commissioned in 1977, the foot of Sutton Mill dam, with its modern weir-top mechanisms for regulating the river's flow marked the limit of the tide. In navigation law, tidal waters are considered to be arms of the sea, so it was to here that the historic limit of public navigation reached.

After it had been brought into operation, the Barrage altered a natural regime, which had dictated events for some twelve thousand years, though it didn't alter the extent of navigation rights. Instead of control by the moon and tides, the rhythm of the river now lay in the hands of engineers in operations rooms, as it took on an expanded role as a source for Yorkshire's drinking water.

A significant part of the river's flow, is now diverted to Elvington and Loftsome Bridge water treatment works. From here it travels through myriads of pipes and domestic taps and toilets before draining through sewerage works and waste water treatment plants into water courses, to eventually reunite with the Derwent's remaining flow somewhere in a mix with the rivers Ouse, Trent and Humber heading downstream.

In 1818, spurred by the economic value of the Derwent Navigation, a canal was opened along the course of the Bielby Beck, from Canal Head at Pocklington to the River Derwent at East Cottingwith, where the old course meets the new. But like the main Derwent Navigation, the arrival of the railways in early Victorian times, crushed any prospect of a continuing profitable use.

When, in 1935, more than 200 years after it was created by Act of Parliament in the reign of Queen Anne, the Statutory Navigation along the river Derwent to Malton and Yedingham, was revoked in the interests of land drainage, navigation rights returned to the status which had existed before 1702.

Navigation on the Pocklington Canal faded too, and in 1968 the canal, which by then had passed into the hands of British Waterways, was designated a Remainder Waterway, where no further treasury funds would be spent to maintain its use.

Over the last thirty years, The Pocklington Canal Amenity Society has sought to restore the canal. Part of it, as far as the village of Melbourne, has been completed. It

is easy to understand the desire to look after this part of our built heritage. But, unfortunately, there are significant potential conflicts between the restoration of the canal and the international nature conservation importance of both the immediate surroundings and the wider Derwent Valley.

Herein lies a dilemma. If the canal isn't managed it will slowly silt up and the wildlife importance will be lost. If it is fully restored it could become a focus for development, with the potential for serious consequential impact on the unspoiled character of the area and its nature conservation interest. But, perhaps there is an answer, which can preserve the historic structures with sensitive management of the waterway habitat, constrained in a way, which can guarantee to restrict levels of use and development. But such a scheme has yet to be explored.

The desire to prevent unwelcome change, which has lain at the heart of efforts to protect the Derwent is also understandable. One of the many remarkable features of the Lower Derwent is the absence of modern developments. Indeed very few structures intrude on the Ings and river landscape, and three of those, Ellerton and Aughton churches and Wressle Castle can hardly be classed as intrusions.

Ellerton and Aughton Churches are two local examples of one of this country's greatest heritage assets. Across the land, churches embody the labours of masons and carpenters over the centuries, as well as an expression of the communities which the churches served, and the people who built and cared for them.

Sadly, in many places, cultural change has rendered many churches poorly attended, inadequately funded and difficult to maintain. In 1978, The Priory Church of St Mary the Virgin and St Lawrence, Ellerton, an early Victorian replacement for a mediaeval predecessor succumbed to redundancy and de-consecration and fell quickly into progressively worsening disrepair. However, all was not lost. Restoration work led by a preservation trust and the community has brought a new and vibrant lease of life. But more of that later.

At All Saints', Aughton, a still used beautiful Norman Church, an Aske (the old English name for a newt) carved into the stonework near the base of its squat, square tower, commemorates a local attorney, Robert Aske, who was ruthlessly and cruelly executed by Henry VIIIth for his leading role in the Pilgrimage of Grace, a northern rebellion against the King's Dissolution of the Monasteries.

Nearby an 11th Century mound marks the place where a wooden Norman keep offered a defensive vantage point over the valley.

A few miles downstream at Wressle, a mediaeval stronghold on a totally different scale, formed part of the Duke of Northumberland's Estates. Around 1380 it was built for Sir Thomas Percy, Earl of Worcester, but much of the castle was destroyed in 1650 during the English Civil War.

Along the river, not far from the castle, under the pressure of the high levels of the river during the floods of 2000, part of the raised flood bank collapsed, inundating an unprecedented area of surrounding land. Only emergency action on a military scale, utilising army Chinook heavy-lifting helicopters to bring in hundreds of used tyres as ballast, managed to stem the flow through the breach.

At Barmby, outside the regulatory control of the Barmby Barrage across the mouth of the Derwent, the River Ouse drains east, joins with the River Trent to become the River Humber, before passing under the sensational Humber Bridge. Now a mile wide, the river flows on past Hull, where slab-sided ferries dominate the daytime scene, past the tiny old Paull lighthouse on the north bank, and oil refineries and Immingham docks on the south. Finally it leaves the estuary between the unique three-mile long Spurn Peninsula and the port of Grimsby. Rain that fell on Fylingdales Moor near Lilla Cross has finally reached the sea.

Grey heron.

Overleaf: *Unspoilt traditional hay meadows full of wildflowers and farmed in a non-intensive way, are the hallmark of the Lower Derwent Valley.*
Page 54: *Proposals to dam and flood upper Farndale to create a reservoir were rejected by Parliament.*

MOMENTS IN TIME

CHAPTER FIVE

Barrage of Criticism

The rejection of plans for a reservoir in Farndale triggered events, which shaped not only the recent history of the river Derwent, but also the lives of people who have fought to protect its future.

It's rather sad that a wonderful river, born tumbling freely across the wildness of the North York Moors, should end its life squeezing between the reinforced concrete and steel-shuttered walls of Barmby Tidal Barrage, a structure with as much charm as an Eastern European border checkpoint in the days of the former Soviet Union.

Why was this necessary and what were the consequences of its construction?

When Richard Watson, the Light Owler Trust's solicitor, as a schoolboy saw a report on the BBC's regional Look North television programme in the late 1960s, he could not have imagined that the story about a reservoir planned for upper Farndale in the North York Moors National Park would influence many aspects of his professional work to support nature conservation a quarter of a century later.

Talking to Richard in his offices in York, he recounted his sense of outrage that the character of Farndale soon would be 'destroyed for ever', such was the typical drama of the news report.

Since 1965, when Sheffield Corporation completed the Elvington Water Treatment Works about a mile upstream of Sutton weir, the notably clean Derwent has been an important source of water for large parts of Yorkshire. But, with burgeoning demands for domestic and industrial supply, far more was required, an impending need forcibly confirmed by the droughts of the mid-1970s and 1990s.

To help to satisfy the growing demand, The Yorkshire Ouse and Hull Rivers Authority, along with Hull and Sheffield Corporations proposed a scheme to increase abstraction through a new water intake and treatment works near to the mouth of the Derwent.

Along with the supply from Elvington, this intake would feed into the Yorkshire Grid and to towns and cities such as Barnsley, Sheffield and Hull.

With about a seventh of Yorkshire ultimately depending on its supply of drinking water from the Derwent, maintaining both quality and quantity was vital. To achieve these standards a number of structures would be required, in addition to the treatment works themselves. To guarantee flows in the river a balancing reservoir to maintain a continuity of levels was proposed. To be located in upper Farndale, it would be formed behind a large sloping earth bank, nearly one hundred and fifty feet high, across part of the valley.

Correspondence with the Rivers Authority at the time records that not everyone was happy with a proposition to radically alter the Moors' most famous Daffodil dale. The letters also show that where change and development come in the countryside, others trying to capitalise on it often follow, an overriding concern to nature conservationists over any major changes to the uses of the River Derwent itself. And long before final decisions were taken, unsolicited approaches for recreational use of the reservoir for water-based activity had already begun.

In the simpler days before the 'death of common sense' and the associated explosion of stifling risk and legal health and safety responsibility issues made it increasingly difficult to do anything involving the public, Yorkshire Water ran its own museum at the appropriately named Springhead Pumping Station, on the outskirts of Hull.

Filled with fascinating material from the past, displayed in a spontaneous way by enthusiasts of the water industry, the historic records and photographs provided a delightfully anachronistic setting for the massive and obsolete, Victorian beam engine-powered pump used to lift water from a cavernous borehole to supply Hull.

Among the exhibits in the engine house, a plan of the proposed Farndale Reservoir Scheme hung on a wall. And as it turned out, that's about as far as it would get - aspirations of engineers, destined to remain a dream.

Another element of the project would be a gauging weir, positioned across the river in the middle reaches. From the flow levels of water across the weir, calculations would determine the rate of release of water from the Farndale reservoir to feed down the Rivers Dove and Rye to maintain the flow in the Derwent.

The final structure required, a set of sluices at the river's mouth, would allow discharge from the Derwent, but prevent saline or polluted water in the River Ouse from flowing back up to contaminate the fresh water to be abstracted at Loftsome Bridge.

With rejection by Parliament alternative provisions to improve water supply had to be devised. In principle, the solution was not radically different in its ultimate practical effect on the lower river.

The Barmby Tidal Barrage Order, confirmed in 1972, reversed the emphasis for controlling river levels. While the scheme would still utilise data from a gauging weir at Buttercrambe to determine the volume of water to be retained in the river, instead of topping up the flow from a reservoir upstream, sophisticated calculations from data gathered at Buttercrambe would govern the timing of opening and closing of a barrage across the river's mouth.

Not long before construction of the Barrage began I had wandered down the bank of the river at Elvington from the village's historic stone bridge to the southern end of the old lock. Looking southwards, the expanses of glistening mud defined a very low tide, the only occasion on which I ever saw the river in this way.

Soon afterwards, the tidal regime would be radically altered, rendering it highly unlikely that within our lifetimes we will ever see the lower reaches in their natural state again.

To accompany the Barrage, a new navigation lock would afford access into the river's publicly navigable stretch and the raising of the river flood banks was also required.

Rudimentary flood banks had lined certain parts of the lower Derwent from at least the 1600s and later evidence of mankind's seemingly eternal desire to tame the flood can also be seen on the early editions of Ordnance Survey maps.

But these and other bank-raising works were judged inadequate to deal with a perceived increased risk of flooding of riverside land from the deployment of the Barrage.

One of the provisions of the Barmby Tidal Barrage Order, known as Clause 13, controversially required a minimum depth of 4 feet to be maintained in the river at all times for the benefit of navigation.

In years to come, this clause would be the subject of much critical questioning, not only about the impacts of its implementation, but also over who had sought to have it included and exactly why, when and how it had been introduced in the first place.

Prior to the commissioning of the barrage, at low water, drainage outfalls from farmland would have been exposed. Now with the proposals to hold the levels artificially some would be submerged, though that did not necessarily mean that they would not still drain to an extent.

Whether a reality, or simply a perception, the farmers of

Top: *The Barmby Tidal Barrage.* Bottom left: *The old Pocklington Canal corridor is a haven for wildlife.*
Bottom right: *Sutton upon Derwent, with its weir, the limit of the tide before the Barmby Tidal Barrage was built across the river's mouth.*

An aerial view of the area between East and West Cottingwith where the Pocklington Canal and Bielby Beck join the River Derwent at the southern end of Yorkshire Wildlife Trust's Wheldrake Ings Nature Reserve. The old course of the river is visible in the centre, at the top.

the Ings were, to say the least, not best pleased. Their displeasure was compounded further when extensive flooding occurred almost immediately after the barrage was brought into action. Firmly believing its operation had caused the problem, they united to challenge its use. Opposition, which, in one form or another, would permeate and influence a succession of events on the river for decades to come.

With the improvement of navigability, coinciding with a national drive for restoration of navigations, interest by boating enthusiasts in the Derwent, began to grow. Historically, it would have been quite an awkward river to enter from the River Ouse, especially with the vagaries of the tide and water depths, but, the inclusion of a lock and the reduction of tidal influences, which would make passage easier, no doubt provided an additional spur to those keen to create and restore the historic navigation.

However, the Derwent's waters were far from calm inside the 'protective' effect of the barrage. The 'uglybirds' of opportunist development had begun to circle. Equally as bad, if you are a nature conservationist, pump-drainage proposals for the meadows, driven in part by the reaction to the flooding, also became an issue. Both posed significant risks for the future of the river, its meadows and wildlife and the character of the countryside on which they depend.

The threats from these harbingers of change are graphically revealed through the plethora of planning applications and works spread between Malton and the Mouth of the River in the mid to late 1970s. Ranging across marinas - four applications, bank-side toilets - four sets, car and caravan parks, moorings and other riverside developments, especially in the lower river and at Stamford Bridge, the multitude of proposals, set alarm bells loudly ringing.

Against this background, anxieties rapidly increased, for the seemingly inexorable slide to wholesale change on the Derwent was gathering pace. Something simply had to be done.

Initial opposition was fragmented. The Derwent Farmers Action Group led by Dave Jackson, founded in May 1977 challenged the operation of the barrage and its impact on agricultural land; the Yorkshire Naturalists Trust (YNT), tormented both the water company and government with incisive questions; the Wildlife Association of the Yorkshire Derwent (WAYD), founded two years earlier in 1975 by angler Cliff Benson, also had support from sporting interests. But, the spur for concerted and firmly focussed action came from another quarter. During restoration of a bridge over the old Pocklington Canal, the road between Sutton upon Derwent and Howden was closed to facilitate works. Giving priority to a barely used and non-essential derelict navigation to the wide-ranging inconvenience of road users, incensed local people, especially some of the villagers in East Cottingwith.

It was then that local farmer, and later to be Parish and District Councillor, Joan Burnett, with fellow farmer Peter Floyd, took up the challenge. Explaining the way she had become involved, Joan described clearly how helpless everyone had felt to begin with, until they gained confidence to assert that these things didn't just have to be accepted – and that something could and would be done. And the rest, as they say, is history.

In June 1977, with representatives from farming, angling and nature conservation interests, the Conservation Society of the Yorkshire Derwent, (CONSYDER), a pressure group, was formed. Guided by Joan as Secretary and supported by Stephen Warburton, this enduring group brought a clear direction to the argument to protect the Derwent.

Looking to avoid reinventing the wheel, CONSYDER modelled its aims on those already established by WAYD two years before. They focussed on: protecting the river system and river life; maintaining cleanliness and minimising pollution; preserving the habitats of species dependent on the river; supporting those responsible for maintaining the natural amenities of the river and promoting greater awareness of the river as a living system.

Perhaps CONSYDER's greatest achievement came in 1978 with publication by the Group of *The Yorkshire River Derwent – A Case for Conservation*. Whatever the promoters of schemes to develop the Derwent thought about the organisation before publication, one thing was abundantly clear from this authoritative report: no one could have been in any doubt that its authors were deadly serious and not likely to give up.

However, matters for CONSYDER could have become complicated. Potential tensions might have emerged through the contradiction for farmers between the proposals for pump drainage to dry land at North Duffield, driven by a response from the Internal Drainage Boards to the perceived impacts of flooding and wetness blamed on the barrage, and the wider fight to protect the Derwent against all unwelcome change. A very tangled web was in danger of being woven, however, luckily, support for pumps was anything but universal within the local farming community.

Farmers, nature conservationists and anglers remained united in their resolve to tackle the root causes of the problems, not just to apply 'successive layers of sticking plaster to a serious wound'. The sense of common purpose for the well-being of the river and its traditional meadows remained intact.

But when a ball starts rolling, it is often difficult to get it to stop.

The Ouse and Derwent Internal Drainage Board's proposed pilot pumping scheme for North Duffield Carrs planned in the late 1970s continued to take shape. If successfully approved and implemented further such schemes were envisaged at Bowthorpe, Menthorpe and Thorganby Ings.

The justification for the proposals, according to an engineer's report completed in August 1983, centred on the assertion that in "the last seven years the level of the River Derwent has consistently failed to fall to such a level to permit the gravity operated clough discharge to function sufficiently to enable the 185 acres of flood plain grassland to be economically used as pasture land or hay-cropping because of the lack of adequate drainage". The proposed solution to the alleged problem was to "install electrically-operated pumps to pump the surplus water into the river Derwent during periods when gravity clough discharge is not possible".

Initially the Nature Conservancy Council (NCC) indicated that it would not object to the scheme, providing certain conditions were met. Later, in the face of further information and developments, the NCC modified its position to one of outright objection.

With a now refined view of the implications of the pumps and their operation, not least who would control them, the NCC determined that "enhanced drainage could potentially lead to agricultural intensification, particularly the conversion of grassland to arable". In the era of subsidy-driven production, such worries throughout the countryside were not without foundation.

Funding was fundamental to the Drainage Board's ability to deliver the project. The Yorkshire Water Authority's Regional Land Drainage Committee (a forerunner of the National Rivers Authority and later Environment Agency) had agreed to contribute significantly to the £60,000 cost of the scheme, on condition that it was approved by the then Ministry of Agriculture Fisheries and Food (MAFF) for 50% grant aid from government.

Conservation interests were resolute in their aim to convince the MAFF of the undesirability of the project, its potentially damaging nature, lack of cost effectiveness and therefore that grant should not be given.

Detailed submissions included an assessment of ornithological importance and risk from change presented by the Royal Society for the Protection of Birds; challenges to the cost benefit assumptions by a leading environmental economist, accompanied by concerted pressure from Stephen Warburton on behalf of the Yorkshire Wildlife Trust..

In 1984, the efforts of objectors bore fruit. The Minister for Agriculture announced the rejection of the application for funding support. Without grant aid, pumps would not be installed; an important precedent had been set. But relief was short-lived. As the sun set on one threat, another, claims for new navigation rights, had already dawned.

Sutton weir, with modern water control mechanisms across its crest and the old lock-keeper's cottage.

Overleaf: *Looking east along the Ings from between Melbourne and Sutton upon Derwent in winter.*

CHAPTER SIX

Purchase and Protect

*International recognition and protective ownership forge an enduring link
between nature conservation and the farmers on which it depends.*

Following a throwaway remark in a previous year's Christmas card, sent by Sarah Priest to four of her former colleagues at the Nature Conservancy Council (NCC), Stephen Ward, Peter Stuttard, Simon Elliott and Tim Dixon, in May 2005 they once more stood out in the meadows where twenty five years before she had worked with them long into evenings and weekends surveying field after field in close detail.

The task had been to record the species composition of wild plants growing across the Ings, a painstaking exercise involving locating and identifying individual species and assessing the density and variety of each within specific areas.

Sarah, Peter and Stephen had undertaken the main field work, Simon dealt with land management issues and Tim provided detailed information on the distribution of bird species using the Ings throughout they year.

Exacting work, undertaken without at the time realising its ultimate significance, as they laid the foundations which, would lead to full formal national and international recognition for the Derwent's habitats and the creation of the Lower Derwent Valley National Nature Reserve (NNR).

In the persistent rain, the former colleagues reflected on the results of their labours. I hope they felt proud. They should have, for a landscape potentially under threat while they compiled new data and collated information from local birdwatchers and naturalists, looked in excellent condition.

However, based in part on their efforts, other wide-ranging changes had occurred to laws and regulations, which help to ensure the quality of the Ings will be sustained. And the Lower Derwent Valley NNR has long been an established part of the local scene.

Without their contributions, driven by personal commitments to safeguard the plants and animals of the Ings, coupled with that of other staff before and since, protecting the area from development from coal mining, drainage and navigation would have been much more difficult, if not impossible to achieve.

Pressure Groups and individual campaigners and conservationists, undoubtedly played an important part in protecting the area. But without the sustained effort to scientifically and legally establish the importance in the first place, coupled with the not inconsiderable and imaginative activity by NCC staff needed to drive it forward, the full formal justification to oppose unwelcome change might not have existed, at least not to anything like the same extent, nor as soon.

In the evening, the wet, weary, though profoundly and rightly content group retired to the St. Vincent Arms in Sutton upon Derwent, a sort of unofficial headquarters and place for celebration by anyone connected with matters Derwent, to reminisce into the night.

As Sarah described the reunion and the extent of the behind the scenes work carried out from her office, I resolved to explore their records where the full extent of the activity required to achieve today's exceptional position would be found.

Simon Christian, who now has a key conservation responsibility for the Lower Derwent Valley for Natural England (NE), greeted me at the office, leading me into a back room, where hundreds of files lined shelf after shelf.

Not long into my journey through this comprehensive record of NE and its predecessors' work, I was already mentally exhausted. How on earth did the authors of all this material ever have the time to write it, let alone deal with matters to which it related, I wondered?

Exploring the grey, buff, blue and pink folders, is not only to take a tour though a mind-boggling array of issues, handled by the staff along the way, but also to meet up again with old friends from the York Office through their signatures on letters and documents spanning the years – Derek Ungley, Michael Woodhouse, Jeff Lunn, Philip Horton, Denise Graham, Sarah Woolven, Denice Leach, Helen 'Brock' Smith, Rex Ireland-Carson, Andy Brown, Richard Rafe and Richard Jefferson to name more than a few. Within the use-worn covers, an official time-line of events unfolds. Knowing what to ignore and what to look for is half of the battle when faced with such overwhelming amounts of detail; avoiding being side-tracked is essential. I was not trying to find out about everything that ever happened here, just the main steps in the evolution of the protected landscapes, a sequence of events, which began at Wheldrake in 1971 when the Yorkshire Naturalists Trust (YNT), bought 270 acres of Wheldrake Ings from the Forbes-Adam family, owners of the Escrick Park Estate.

Motivation for the acquisition had centred on the possibility of drainage and agricultural intensification, incompatible with the ornithological interests of the site,

and also the desire to reduce the disturbance to wintering wildfowl by visitors coming to see the spectacle.

It had long been known that the area was home, especially in winter when the land floods, to large numbers of wildfowl and swans, especially Bewick's and whooper swans, whose breeding grounds lay in the Arctic across Greenland, Iceland and northern Scandinavia and Russia.

A year later, the YNT acquired a further large parcel of land known as North Hill Ings, historically part of West Cottingwith Ings, bringing its total land ownership in the valley to some 400 acres.

Some of the early priorities for the site included increasing the amount of water in the early part of the bird-breeding season along with reducing visitor disturbance of wintering birds. Permanent open water was also created. With the assistance of the army a large pond with convoluted margins and shallow gradients covering several acres was excavated in the centre of the site. Strategic drainage ditches were filled with concrete to impede the discharge of water, though in time these obstructions were removed to allow better management of water when its release needed to be carefully controlled. Water control mechanisms, know as Cloughs, were also constructed on main drainage ditches to manage the water levels more readily.

In the early 1970s none of the land in the Derwent Valley enjoyed any statutory protection. While concerted efforts were being made to benefit birds, the species-rich grasslands, themselves dependent on highly specific conditions, had not enjoyed attention to the same degree.

That a similar emphasis was not given to the plants at the outset is not surprising. The scale of threat to habitats from conversion to intensively farmed arable and grassland throughout the United Kingdom was not so keenly recognised then and the thrust of the conservation movement to protect what remained was still in its infancy.

In its quest to reduce disturbance, the YNT was fortunate that no public rights of way crossed its Ings land. At least the control of all access lay firmly in the Trust's hands.

Stimulated by the land acquisitions, more extensive and detailed assessments of the whole of the Lower Derwent Valley's habitats and its wildlife followed.

As a result, in 1975, several areas of the Derwent Ings were notified as Sites of Special Scientific Interest (SSSI) under the provisions of the 1949 National Parks and Access to the Countryside Act. What makes this defining legislation all the more remarkable is its timing. In a country exhausted by the effects of the Second World War, with rationing still widespread, Parliament nevertheless had the will, energy and perspicacity to lay the foundations for our national parks and protection and enjoyment of the countryside.

Initially, the discrete areas notified as SSSIs covered Wheldrake Ings, East Cottingwith Ings, Aughton Ings, North Duffield Carrs and Bubwith Ings. In 1981 the boundary was extended to encompass wider areas, to be called collectively The Derwent Ings SSSI.

Two years later all of the land holdings within the SSSIs were re-notified under the provisions of the 1981 Wildlife and Countryside Act. This brought strengthened protection and financial resources for farmers to be compensated for not intensifying the use of land to the detriment of nature conservation. Known as Section 15 Agreements, after a relevant part of an earlier Act of Parliament, which had established the principle, they formed the basis from which the later, more positively slanted Wildlife Enhancement Scheme to support farmers' conservation work, evolved.

By 1985, the network of protected meadows and pastures had been further extended to include Melbourne and Thornton Ings, along the course of the Old Pocklington Canal, Breighton Meadows at the southern end of the Ings and at Newton Mask, an isolated area some four miles upstream to the north, near Newton upon Derwent.

At about the same time, the river itself was notified as an SSSI.

The Ings might be wonderful for wildife, but without the application of chemicals and artificial fertilisers or conversion to other uses they offered a limited financial return for their owners.

Faced with large areas of economically poor land, farmers understandably sought to maximise any income from it through agreements with the NCC. In the face of the financial realities, staff at the NCC took an imaginative step.

During 1982, approval was sought to buy land in the valley with the first acquisition at Aughton Ings. The justification was three-fold: it made economic sense to buy rather than pay annually for agreements; improved conservation management could be put in place and farmers could benefit from an immediate capital sum, while still being able to lease-back the land, and vitally for nature conservation, continue their traditional association with the Ings as part of their farm businesses. Though, from the outset, it was never the intention to purchase more than a part of the Ings land.

When the original land acquisition strategies were being developed, the YNT, NCC and The Royal Society for the Protection of Birds (RSPB), had sought a three-way approach to potential land purchases. Each organisation would focus on a third of the Ings, split on a north-south basis.

As it turned out, the RSPB didn't proceed, believing its best interest lay elsewhere in England, but the YNT did add a number of smaller meadows to its land holding. The rest of the initiative primarily lay with the NCC.

Parcel by parcel, additional land was brought into protective ownership. With eventually more than a thousand acres under NCC control, the final part of the vision could be brought into play.

In 1990, large sections of the Lower Derwent Valley, a mosaic of conservation organisation land holdings, spread between other privately owned Ings land, were designated an NNR. This included YWT's Wheldrake Ings and all of the NCC's holdings.

The following year, in a two part ceremony, split between an on site event at Bank Island, where the Reserve was dedicated to the outgoing Chairman of the NCC, Sir William Wilkinson, and an indoor event at Bubwith, the

The Derwent Ings through the seasons, each photograph taken from the same place on the old Pocklington Canal towpath near Melbourne.
Top row across the double spread: *January, February, March, April, May and June …*

Bottom row across the double spread: ... *July, August, September, October, November and December.*

NNR was formally opened on Thursday 14 March 1991, by The Rt. Hon. The Earl of Cranbrook the Chairman designate of English Nature, NCC's successor organisation,

In a symbolic gesture, the international connections of the site were reinforced through special guest Dr Andrey Vinokurov from the All-Union Institute for Nature Conservation, Moscow.

The opening of the NNR was a crowning occasion for the Derwent Valley and a ringing endorsement to the labours of NCC's staff who had steered it into being.

With complex land-ownership patterns of fields spread in mosaics across the floodplain, and the clear need to minimise disturbance, public facilities for enjoyment posed a number of problems.

Focussing on key locations for access proved the perfect solution. This way, disturbance in the sanctuary areas over wide parts of the reserve could be kept to a minimum, while the public could still readily enjoy strategically placed hides and viewing points. These facilities were located at Wheldrake Ings, at Bank Island, near Wheldrake and at North Duffield Carrs, with a later viewing point created behind the car park at Thorganby Village Hall.

At North Duffield, a hide and scrape, a shallow pool with wide muddy margins, were constructed in 1987 and 1988 to encourage feeding wading birds The hide is dedicated to the memory of Geoff Smith, a local ornithologist, who died relatively young. Much of his bird recording work underpinned the initial appreciation of the importance of the Derwent Valley for its birds, on which the decisions to acquire particular land holdings were based.

There are of course many individuals who have played their parts, not least Tim Dixon, who had steered the construction of the hide and organised the ceremony of celebration.

I had first met Tim when Stephen Warburton and I were battling to save heather moorlands, in the North York Moors, from being ploughed up and Tim had come to confirm that nightjars were breeding on a particular moor.

During the formative years of the Derwent's growing importance, the designations and ultimately the arrival of the NNR, Tim had been firstly a volunteer, then a contract warden and finally the Site Manager for the NNR, before moving on to work in Herefordshire. His place was taken by Peter Roworth, formerly the Site Manager at Thorne and Hatfield Moors NNR.

The full extent of the protected areas along the Lower Derwent now covered some 2400 acres, the largest area of unimproved traditional floodplain haymeadows in the country.

With increased knowledge of the Derwent's birds, its grasslands and wetlands and the value of the river, other accolades followed.

Firstly, the Ings were designated a Ramsar Wetland of International Importance and an European Union Special Protection Area for Birds (SPA), followed by designation as a European Union Special Area of Conservation (SAC) for its rare grasslands, otters and alder woods. One of the types of grassland, sounding more like a make of car that a rare wildlife habitat and known as MG4, is only found in the United Kingdom. Of this rare resource a large proportion lies in the Derwent Valley. And the river, itself designated an SSSI, was also notified as a SAC, a move, which would lead to legal action over the operation of the Barmby Tidal Barrage.

While much of the major conservation activity centred on the Lower Derwent, other parts of the river system have not been overlooked in establishing their status for nature conservation. Large parts of the North York Moors are also an SSSI, an SPA and an SAC; Duncombe Park and Forge Valley and Raincliffe Woods are SSSIs and NNRs; and Jeffry Bog, and Kirkham Park and riverside are also SSSIs.

From very basic beginnings, within twenty years, important aspects of the River and its surroundings had moved from barely any protection to extensive recognition of their international standing.

Top left: *Sarah Priest, second from the right in red, explains the management of grasslands.*
Top right: *Aeshna dragonfly.* Bottom left: *Pochard.* Bottom centre: *Frog.* Bottom right: *Great burnet.*

Overleaf: *The Derwent's peaceful character inspired anglers, nature conservationists and riparian owners in their campaign to keep the river free from inappropriate development and intrusive uses.*

CHAPTER SEVEN

Challenges in Court

A challenge in the High Court sees landowners, farmers, fishermen and conservationists united in defence of a national test case to protect the river from the risk of change.

Remarkably, the most significant issue for the River Derwent – a High Court Action over navigation rights - barely features in the official files at Natural England, the successor to English Nature (EN).

Although the matter ground on for fifteen years, with claims, counter claims and court hearings, the proceedings lay beyond the scope of EN's responsibilities. It wasn't that their staff were disinterested, but simply that all nature conservation designations and regulations are subservient to the law of the land on public rights of way and the extent of the public rights of navigation were in dispute.

Since 1935, when the statutory navigation, created in the early 18th Century, was extinguished, aspirations to re-open the river under a new regime had arisen from time to time. In 1959, a navigation restoration organisation was established to seek to acquire the navigation rights, which were recognised as resting with the riverside owners above Sutton upon Derwent.

Twelve years later, invigorated by the spirit of the times, a newly incorporated organisation called the Yorkshire Derwent Trust Limited (YDT), acquired a lease, which later lapsed, on the old lock structure at Elvington, one of several which passed into the ownership of the Catchment Board and its successors after the revocation of the statutory navigation in 1935. The YDT aimed to install new gates and restore the two-hundred-year old lock chamber to working order as the first stage of a plan to re-open the river to through navigation upstream from the limit of the tidal reaches at Sutton upon Derwent.

Amidst local publicity, Elvington lock re-opened in the summer of 1972, but the proposed use of the river led to objections and considerable obstacles for the promoters of the navigation lay ahead. While boating interests claimed a through right of navigation existed to Malton and beyond, many riparian (riverside) owners, nature conservationists and anglers did not agree with their view that it extended that far.

To make a clear point, Stephen Warburton, arranged for colleagues from the Yorkshire Naturalists Trust to help riparian owners to erect notices on their land pointing out the position. The opening shots in a protracted confrontation had been fired and a sustained battle over the river's future use had begun.

Subsequently, the Conservation Society for the Yorkshire Derwent (CONSYDER), following its publication of *The River Derwent – A Case for Conservation*, wrote to riparian owners pointing out the implications of the growing demand for boating and associated developments on the river.

Matters came to a head in 1980, when supporters of

the YDT proposed to run boat trips between Malton and Kirkham. Whether they were intended to or not, the planned trips forced the issue over the question of the right of navigation along these reaches.

Riparian owners on both banks between Huttons Ambo and Kirkham objected. Permission could well have been given for the trips if it had been sought by the organisers, but it was not. In the end the boat trips were cancelled.

The owners of the riparian rights had been put in an invidious position. On the face of it, to object to the use of one small boat with proceeds to support local charities might seem unduly churlish. But to not to do so would have been to accept the principle that a general right of navigation existed, with the way then being open for that right to be exploited, placing potential new pressures on the river.

In this it is important to recognise that the public right of navigation and numbers of vessels using it cannot be restricted easily. A right for one boat is a right for all and as many as want to come, from canoe to the largest vessel that can navigate the water, subject only to reasonableness.

All went quiet. That is, until May 1984, when the four riparian owners who had objected to the boat trips, were served with a summons in the name of "The Attorney General at and by the Relation of the Yorkshire Derwent Trust Limited and Malton Town Council". Accompanying, the summons, a large pile of documents purporting to prove that the river had been a public navigation since time immemorial, backed up the wide-ranging claims. Someone had clearly not been idle in the intervening four years.

It wasn't that objectors to navigation on the Derwent were against the general principle of people enjoying boats, only that they believed this was not the place to develop boating, when so many less environmentally sensitive alternatives exist.

If the substantial bundle of complex documents was meant to frighten everyone into submission, it didn't work.

Instead, pre-existing links between individuals and organisations keen on retaining the status quo on the river, were simply reinforced and galvanised into a closely cooperative response.

The unusual legal mechanism chosen to bring the case to court is known as a Relator Action. Brought in the name of the Attorney General on behalf of the public as the Plaintiff – the person making the claim - but linked to those behind the issue to be determined, in this instance the Yorkshire Derwent Trust Ltd and Malton Town Council, it was, from their point of view, a sensible route to take.

If the claim had been brought against the riverside owners by the YDT and the Town Council acting alone, the outcome would only have established the position between the two sides in the case. By involving the Attorney General, the result would be binding on all society for all time. That is of course if the Attorney General won, as usually he is expected to do in such matters, when normally the device is used for 'mopping-up', to bring legal clarity to an issue. Even the legal rules and guidance did not contemplate that the Attorney General could ever lose or be responsible for any costs if he did. But this would prove to be a rather more complicated affair.

The case would be heard in the Chancery Division of the High Court in London. Before that, many time-consuming procedural steps lay ahead. In short, though in practice their progress spanned months and years rather than weeks, the elaborate procedure unfolded.

Firstly, the Attorney General sought a declaration that there was a public right of navigation for the public in all types of vessels past the land of the defendants, the riparian owners, and that such through right existed to Malton and beyond.

The initial legal step in response involved seeking further and better particulars. An application to the court to join in two extra Defendants, followed, the Yorkshire Wildlife Trust, owner of a nature reserve alongside the river at Jeffry Bog in the northern end of Kirkham Gorge, and the

Aldby Park Estate, which had judiciously managed access to its stretch of the river at Buttercrambe.

Points of Claim and Points of Defence had to be clarified and set down precisely. These would be followed by further Pleadings to the Court; each step backed up by numerous and extensive written affidavits setting out the evidence to support both sides' cases.

A senior partner in Leeds Solicitors, Hepworth and Chadwick, Howard Bryan, originally responsible for the case, had handed it over to Paul Smith, who had come to the firm from working for the solicitors to the Bank of England in London, with the throwaway remark: "this looks as if it might run for some while. You're young, so better you do it so you don't run out of time"; prophetic words indeed. We would all be ten years older and substantially wiser when the job was finally done. Even more prophetically, Howard suggested that the issue had the potential to go all the way to the House of Lords.

I once asked Paul how he coped with such labyrinthine procedures. "The number one rule, before anything else is that you've got to be good at efficiently managing paper. If you can't do that, forget it" he replied. To back up the Defendants, the River Derwent Appeal Group (The Group) formed, bringing together a small number of people who had worked together over the years. The Group changed little during the course of the case and provided a clear focus and continuity to the efforts to defend the action.

It mattered little that this was one of the best rivers in the country for wildlife. Regrettably, for all of us, the issue could only be fought through property ownership, as fundamentally English Law is there to protect private property rights not to arbitrate over competing public interests.

The Group ultimately comprised: Anne Henson and Mark Winn as representatives of the riparian owners, Ian Kibble, formerly Chief Executive of the Yorkshire Wildlife Trust and subsequently Regional Director of the Country Landowners Association; Andrew Dudley-Smith –

Regional Director of the National Farmers' Union, Joan Burnett, farmer, founding member of CONSYDER and the Chairman of the Group; Stephen Warburton representing the Yorkshire Wildlife Trust, and Rocky Lee of York Amalgamation of Anglers.

Although invited to be a part of the Group, I declined. As I would be devising and directing the fund-raising and public relations, and ultimately along with Stephen, the preparatory research for the evidence, it felt important not to participate in the decisions as to how to spend the money as well.

Throughout the case the Group met regularly in the offices of the NFU at Murton, near York, to keep a tight grip on the course of events. Meetings were always low on debate and high on clear courses of action. That's the beauty of small committees of focussed people. Charting our way through the Courts, would take as circuitous a journey as the river itself, while years evaporated and the paper mountain grew through the progress of numerous pre-hearings and exchanges of affidavits.

The claim for public rights of navigation embraced several permutations as to how such a right might exist. It felt like being in a horse race where many horses are running against you, with the Plaintiffs only needing one to get home to succeed.

Firstly, there was the assertion that the right of navigation had always existed along the whole river from time immemorial. Then, if not that, that it was created in the 1702 River Derwent Navigation Act, but had not been taken away when the statutory navigation had been revoked in 1935; or, that if that hadn't happened it had arisen between 1702 and 1935 because vessels had used the river; or that it had arisen since 1935. Important to other claims later in the case, would be the interpretation of the 1932 Rights of Way Act, 1949 National Parks and Access to the Countryside Act, and 1959 and 1980 Highways Acts and what each of those meant, as far as a claim for navigation rights through long-user are concerned.

Top left: *The author launches the River Derwent Appeal for funds to defend the river in the courts by collecting a lucky pot of Derwent water.*
Top right: *The Campaign Prospectus, a fundamental tool towards raising nearly £600,000.* Bottom left: *The World Wide Fund For Nature sends a Panda.* Bottom right: *Well-known TV botanist of the time, David Bellamy lends a hand.*

Faced with so many issues, the Defendants applied for a split trial. This made both practical and economic sense. If one of the preliminary points were to be lost, then wasting time and money on later issues would be senseless. The courts agreed and the issues to be determined distilled to five key Preliminary Issues to be tried. Four of the points dealing with various historic and legal events would determine the status of navigation rights on the river, immediately after the River Derwent Navigation Revocation Order was confirmed on 23 September 1935, and the fifth, the true meaning of the 1932 Rights of Way Act and subsequent Highways Acts, a point not only of fundamental importance to any remaining issues to be considered on the River Derwent after 1935, but also to rivers throughout England and Wales.

Getting to the court doors had been a formidable task for both sides. From here it would be equally arduous with long hearings in each of The High Court, Court of Appeal and House of Lords, as well as other associated presentations and submissions, including those to the House of Lord's Appeal Committee and for the making of Directions and Orders for Costs.

Ably led by Paul Smith, Stephen and I, as novices, were on the steep learning curve of a hands-on experience taking us through every step in the processes of the highest courts in the land, not one you would readily wish to repeat.

But the legal dimensions, demanding as they might have been, were only one of three planks in the collective efforts. The other two, fund-raising - this was going to cost a lot of money and you needed to raise double in case you lose – and the press and publicity activity, would be every bit as taxing; they would be interesting, pressured and sometimes highly entertaining experiences in their own right.

Otter.

Overleaf: *A sudden late summer flood catches out the farmer just north of Buttercrambe bridge.*

CHAPTER EIGHT

Getting an Act Together

Thousands of hours of historical research reveal remarkable details of events stretching back a thousand years.

Time was running out. A September deadline for the submission of a response to the claim loomed. Little progress had been made. Approaches to historians in a quest to find a specialist who could help to provide the answers had proved fruitless.

One afternoon in frustration, I took all the court papers to Stephen's house in York. We agreed that we needed to take a good look at the documents ourselves. Settling down with a bottle of sherry, hundreds of pages of dense reading stretched before us; it would be a long night.

We both grew increasingly despondent. Page after page of the evidence submitted to support the claim seemed to our non-legal eyes, to confirm extensive use of the river for navigation in past centuries, very different to the character of the river as we thought we knew it and long before the present disagreements and court action began.

We knew we needed to tackle it, but where were we to start?

To begin with, a few ground rules were set. Research would concentrate on trying to counter the information presented by the Plaintiffs by leaving no stone unturned in a drive to enhance our understanding of the river in the past. At the same time, we agreed not to be economical with the truth. If the results of the research turned out badly, we would face up to it, hard as that might be.

We also established that we would both work on the submissions in response, with me drafting and Stephen challenging and refining, then pass our preliminary material onto Paul Smith and David Ainger, the Defendants' Barrister, who would lead the case in court, to edit, expand and turn it into an appropriate legal form. Stephen would sign the affidavits, leaving me free to handle the public face of the campaign without compromising our position in court.

My first research trip to The House of Lords library was daunting. There, lined up on the shelves, row after row of Journals of the House of Commons and House of Lords, recorded seemingly endless details of procedural debate and legislation.

Initial investigation centred on the background to Acts of Parliament in 1696 and 1698, which had been claimed by the Plaintiffs to precede the Act of 1702 to make the Derwent – then spelt Darwent – navigable.

The index to the journals recorded numerous references to a River Derwent at the end of the 17th Century, but not any of that date related to the river in Yorkshire.

It then dawned on me that the evidence was wrong; the Plaintiff's had mixed up the Yorkshire and Derbyshire Derwents. I telephoned Stephen. We were both greatly encouraged. It was only a very small and inconsequential point, but if this could be wrong, what else might we discover?

This easily made mistake, taught us an important lesson: never to rely on received wisdom or secondary sources, always go back to the originals. Not only might they say something different, but often they also contain other associated and useful facts.

The Plaintiffs had relied on a published book, the author of which had made the error and they had presented his account in their evidence as though it were correct.

Back in the library, I subsequently found several entries in the Journals for the Yorkshire Derwent, including for a Bill which had begun its passage in 1701 before the death of King Wiliam III, progressing to an Act being passed in 1702, during the first year of the reign of Queen Anne.

In a stroke of luck, I then chanced upon a vital piece of evidence. A petition to Parliament in 1722 complaining about the charges for the navigation, revealed how users of the rivers viewed the situation at the turn of the seventeenth century. From the complaints, it was clear that Sutton had been as far up river as they were accustomed previously to be able to freely navigate. In a further twist, an entry in an adjacent column caught my eye. A name, Jon Jenyns, a very similar name to one of the principal Defendants and riparian owners John Jenyns, jumped out at me. In all those pages, in all those hundreds of books spanning Britain's Parliamentary History, an unusually spelt name with a close connection appeared virtually next to one of the defining pieces of evidence in support of our case.

I never did get round to asking John whether there was a family connection, but I took it as a good sign, an omen confirming we were heading in the right direction; that somehow everything was going to be alright.

Photocopies were needed and needed fast. It would be a common problem over the next five years. Copies could be ordered, but it was often difficult to get them immediately. In The House of Lords Library I explained to the librarian that the copies were needed urgently for a court case. Now, mention court cases or legal action in places like this and local records offices and for some reason you hit a wall of bureaucracy and procedures. However, this time we were lucky, the librarian was a member of a local wildlife trust.

When he found out why we needed them the tenor of the conversation immediately changed.

"Let me see, what do you need? I'll nip round the back and copy it now for you and anything else you need", he suggested enthusiastically. I was greatly relieved

Encouraged by the results of the early research, our confidence grew and a plan for information gathering hatched. The tactics were simple but effective. Armed with a list of key place names along the river, Stephen and I attacked the indexes of archive collections and books. Relevant page references were noted, to be investigated in full at a later date.

We recorded anything that might be remotely useful. We scoured Pipe Rolls, Calendar of Letters Patent, Coram Rege Rolls, Charter Rolls, Surtees Society Records, Yorkshire Fines, York Archaeological and Philosophical Society publications, House of Commons Journals, House of Lords Journals and every possible book that might yield evidence. The same intense effort, we unleashed on the Public Records Office and County Records Offices catalogues, Ordnance Survey offices and libraries, continually expanding the resource of references. Spreading from London to Edinburgh, Sheffield, Beverley, Hull, Northallerton, Nottingham, Derby, Norwich, Southampton and York, anything with the remotest possible link, we sought out from estate records, Inclosure Awards, 1910 Finance Act documents, railway plans, river authority and council minutes, rates returns, Hansard reports and the background to making of Acts and Orders of Parliament.

The growing pile of paper filled dozens of legal boxes, all the time building up an impression of the life and times of the river. Importantly and thankfully, in all the historic information nothing contradicted the Defendants' point of view.

Newspapers proved another exceptional source of information. The idea to investigate them sprang from reading a collection of press cuttings, given to me by Sydney Jameson, who I had met some years before on Butterwick Bridge. As a correspondent for the local paper,

Top left: *Celebrating the Defendants' first affidavit evidence at Sutton mill dam (clockwise from back left) Jan Knowlson, Stephen Warburton, Margaret Wolstenholme, Richard Groom, Ian Kibble, Peter Floyd, Elaine Blake, the Author, Joan Burnet, Gannet the greyhound, Tim Dixon.*
Top right: *Tim Dixon mixes it with a lamprey at Buttercrambe.* Bottom left: *A Luftwaffe photograph taken on 4th October 1939 showing the centre of Malton.* Bottom right: *Stephen Warbuton reflects on events in the St Vincent Arms.*

Left: *Margaret Wolstenholme, delivering the Premier Performance of her 'Derwent Song', the words of which are shown on page 142.*
Top right: *Job done – Paul Smith swamped by a pile of paper in his office.*
Bottom right: *Stephen Warburton and the author literally taking cases to court.*

Sydney had written extensively about local events throughout the 1930s. Some of his pieces contained photographs and descriptions of activity on and around the local rivers. One even had a picture of an otter hunt on the River Rye.

This sparked further lines of enquiry. Two journalists, Margaret Wolstenholme and Richard Groom, who worked for the Malton Gazette and Herald and Yorkshire Evening Press respectively, arranged for us to borrow the papers' clippings files. Kept for stories that run and run, of which the Derwent navigation saga was clearly one, the archive charted its progress, recounting what had happened and who had said what since 1970.

Laura Wiles, a colleague of Stephen's at the Yorkshire Wildlife Trust then delved deeply into a century's worth of back issues, reading every one and picking up snippets of relevant information from Malton newspapers published back into the 19th Century. The letters pages and public notices were often the most rewarding.

The timing was fortunate. Not long after our comprehensive search, microfiche took over. Scanning a hundred years worth of newspapers in bound volumes might seem a formidable undertaking; using microfilm readers to cover the same ground would have proved an impossible task.

Sydney's cuttings, especially the one about the otter hounds, triggered another idea. A bird-watching friend, Heather Reynolds, whose father was a Malton solicitor, councillor and a keen amateur film maker and otter hunt supporter, held his extensive collection of old 16mm films and 35mm negatives. Many of Malton town and the river, also dated back into the 1930s to the end of the era of the statutory navigation.

With a home-made apparatus to wind the reels, we had no film projector, every single film frame was inspected under a magnifying glass, to see what was happening in the background in the scenes. It was occasionally difficult not to be distracted by other subjects, notably when a blaze was created to test fire fighting equipment on the banks of the river, and when elephants came to town. There was also a fine collection of 'VE' Day activities in Malton.

Aerial photographs and maps would also play a part. A Luftwaffe spy photograph taken on the 4th October 1939, obtained from the archives of the United States; RAF surveys in 1946; early Aerofilms photographs from the 1920s; items from Cambridge University collection, and more modern images from the Ordnance Survey and North Yorkshire County Council, each gave a snapshot in time of the position on the river. A complete up-to-date aerial sequence of the length of the river from Malton to Wheldrake Ings was also taken at the outset of the preprations for the case.

All contained useful information. Most intriguing however, was the 1946 RAF photograph of Kirkham, in which a rectangular area stood out in the pasture between the ruined Abbey and the river. We puzzled over the feature, which can no longer be seen. Only subsequently did we discover its covert purpose, as a testing 'tank', through which vehicles, covered in a top-secret coating could be driven under water.

Full sets of the first edition of Ordnance Survey 25 inch and 6 inch maps of the river and data from the 1910 Finance Act materials covering the entire riverside were obtained.

The Finance Act, often called the Second Domesday of England, which was never implemented, provided for surveys of all landed property in the country as a precursor to levying rates. The surveys comprised three components: hereditament maps showing each property; field books describing details of the land, and the so-called Domesday Books with a catalogue of the assessments. Within these data, information about public rights of way and other easements would be recorded. At the time it was not generally known that these are public documents. Requests of the local District Valuer's Office to let you see the maps was not especially welcomed by office staff, who seemed uncomfortable and certainly hesitant when requested to produce them. After the experiences with records offices over material for evidence in a court case, we never explained why we wanted them and brass-necked persistence was required.

When Tim Dixon visited the Hull office to transcribe details of scores of land holdings onto copy maps standing at the counter, he wasn't even offered a seat or a table.

But not everywhere was like this by any means. By way of contrast, when running out of time at the Public Record Office staff literally took him by the hand and hurried him though the building to find the records he sought.

Similar help was forthcoming at the Borthwick Institute of Historical Research in York, where Chris Webb, a historian and a committed supporter of the campaign to protect the river, produced dozens of historic Inclosure and Tithe maps for inspection, under the Institute's advanced booking system. Research, which would have taken days, ordering materials at three items a time on an ordinary visit, was instead completed in a few hours.

The Wentworth Woodhouse Muniments in Sheffield Library, Aldby Park and other estate records in North Yorkshire County Records Office and Howsham, Wressle and Catton Estates at the Humberside County Record Office all became familiar territory.

One of the most unusual experiences involved looking at the Deposited Plans for the making of the York and Scarborough Railway in the early 1840s. The original documents were housed in British Rail's central archives in York. These maps showed not only the centre line for the proposed railway, but the area of deviation to either side into which the construction might shift to deal with the practical and engineering subtleties on the ground. Equally as important as the map, the schedule of parcels of land over which the line might impinge included a list of those with a legal interest and whether public rights of way, including public navigation rights, might be involved. We were particularly interested in the places where the railway ran near to or crossed the river. Nothing adverse to our position was found.

The archive rooms, which lay in the basement of the magnificent North Eastern Railway building in York, exuded an atmosphere of an old underground station, quite separate from the everyday world of the offices upstairs.

Our rapidly expanding collection of material had become overwhelming. Much of it in old documents proved difficult to read and needed transcription. Hour after hour, Stephen screwed up his eyes, interpreted what he saw and I typed. All of this, just to get to the starting gate. But the intense research helpfully meant we could talk and think and debate events in the language of our own world, bridging the centuries on the Derwent. At times it was almost as if we were actually there, seeing places and events as people of their times might have seen and talked about them.

We had information, enormous amounts of it. Now we had to marshal the arguments to counter the claims, or get someone to do it for us.

I visited Colin Seymour, with whom Stephen had worked on other campaigning projects. Colin, a formidable opponent to those whom he sought to challenge, an expert on the provisions of Highways Acts, the Enclosure Awards and one of Britain's most successful litigants-in-person was a known force to be reckoned with. It was a good job he supported our work.

Colin looked carefully through the lever-arch files.

Mindful of Paul Smith's view about success being linked to the ability to organise paper, great care had been taken over the presentation of the documents.

"Don't worry any more about looking for experts to help you– do it yourselves" Colin advised firmly.

I returned home, took his advice and Stephen and I wrapped the metaphoric cold wet towels around our heads and set about the task. With one month to go to the September deadline, prepapration of the Defendants' first affidavit was finally underway.

At this stage, in the late summer of 1985, we were content solely with putting forward a credible response to the initial claim to avoid running out of time. Refining matters could come later. Our preliminary drafts were forwarded to Paul Smith and David Ainger who developed them into a professional legal format.

The Plaintiffs were pressing for our reply. We sensed

that they imagined we would not manage to make an adequate response, or any response at all, especially as it was reported in the newspapers that we'd left it too late.

Always with an eye for a sense of occasion, we were determined to complete the evidence so that Stephen could swear the first affidavit on 23 September 1985, 50 years to the day since the statutory navigation was revoked.

We put the final touches to it it late that afternoon and I left Paul and Stephen to have it sworn. What they didn't tell me until some time later is that they couldn't find a solicitor to swear it before so late in the evening of the 23rd; it was in fact completed on the morning of the 24th. But it was done in time and a critical milestone had been successfully reached.

Although the first affidavit had been deposited, there would be no real respite, though the pressure for research eased a little. That is, until just before Christmas 1985, when a Notice to Admit Facts served on the Defendants by the Plaintiffs' solicitors, set a time limit of seven days in which to reply. Annoyingly, the supporting papers behind the Notice would be made available for inspection at the Plaintiff's solicitor's offices in London, but not copies to bring back for careful consideration in Leeds. The timing, with a deadline running into Christmas and with the documents 200 miles away, seemed designed to make life difficult.

The team moved back into top gear, brought forward the completion of the next affidavit containing new information which had been discovered, and arranged for Stephen and Colin Seymour to make the journey to London to inspect the files.

With a Christmas party getting under way, minds at the Plaintiff's solicitors were on other things. A clerk ushered them into a room, provided the documents and left them alone. They worked quickly. With their inspection complete, Stephen produced a gift-wrapped parcel of new evidence. Explaining it was a present in return for their clients, he handed it over to the clerk, as they left. But they did not leave empty-handed, the relevant contents from all of the papers, which they had viewed, had been dictated onto tape or photographed to enable the lawyers and the rest of the team to consider them at leisure back at home.

A similar tightly-timed manoeuvre to the Notice to Admit Facts occurred in the run-up to the trial, when another sizeable affidavit was served on the Defendants, leaving little opportunity to respond as the hearing loomed.

Above: *Yellow flag*. Overleaf: *The river that hopes for tranquillity.*

CHAPTER NINE

Battle of the Evidence

Three major trials in the High Court, Court of Appeal and House of Lords explore the Derwent's past.

On 28th June 1988, in the Royal Courts of Justice in the Strand, the long awaited River Derwent Court Case opened. In the light of the large quantity of new evidence recently served on the Defendants by the Plaintiffs, the Judge, Mr Justice Vinelott, offered the Defendant's the option for a postponement of the trial. The offer was declined. It was time to 'get on with the job and absorb the pressure'; structuring any response would be tackled as the case advanced. Everyone, including the judge, looked relieved.

At the outset, the judge defined his limits for the historic part of the case.

"The Plaintiffs have invited me to delve back into the mists of time in the Iron Age. I do not think it helpful to go back so far; I will begin at Domesday", he explained precisely. It seemed he was about to enjoy himself.

Court cases are often won, not on what is presented beforehand, but by how you cope with the questions which arise during the trial. Paul had advised us carefully on being prepared. We were as ready as we could be, with Stephen in court acting as the link-man to the legal team, base-camp, established in Butterwick, as a focus for rapid-response research to solve any issues raised by the judge and practical and specialist supporters ready to help at a moment's notice. We even had a system planned, if we needed to turn to 24 hour working.

Simultaneously carrying out research, preparing court documents, raising money and handling the public relations had been tough going. But we had a few secret weapons to help to lighten the load. Alongside our specialist supporters a regular contribution from unlikely quarters was always welcome.

Chris Yates, a long-time friend and renowned angler, proclaimed an ability to communicate with Izaak Walton, the 17th Century writer of the Compleat Angler, so that he would keep an eye out for us and lend a celestial guiding hand from time to time. It started as a bit of fun, but after a few remarkable coincidences stemming from a 'Message from Izaak', we ritually 'got in touch' when no better way of coming to a decision could be found.

It worked like this. Chris put a couple of marbles in his eye sockets and made funny noises as if communing with one step beyond. He would then pronounce that we would receive a sign at a certain time. Elaine Blake, another friend would be despatched to look out for a sign and if she felt she had spotted one we would go with the advice which Chris had arrived at for us using a Decision Coin. The copper coin depicted the words 'Do it' and an image of a pixie on a toad-stool one side and on the other 'leave it' with a picture of the devil. On such a flimsy basis were some very tricky decisions made, both before and during the Trial.

Opening their submissions, each barrister in turn - Bill Christie, for the Plaintiffs (The Attorney General, Yorkshire

Derwent Trust Ltd – the navigation interests - and Malton Town Council), and David Ainger for the Defendants (representing nature conservationists, anglers, farmers and riparian owners) - worked methodically through their respective cases. Every time the court went into recess, Stephen phoned through a detailed report.

The weather turned extremely hot, especially in central London. So hot, that at one point, the judge ordered that wigs could be removed. This worried Paul. He didn't like it when judges found it too hot and took their wigs off, in case they ceased to think straight.

If the case was complicated before the hearing began, once the debate, argument and counter-argument started in earnest, it ascended to even more complex and still higher intellectual heights.

The Plaintiffs firstly sought to prove that there had always been a historic public right to navigate the length of the river from its mouth at Barmby upstream to Yedingham and beyond – the First Preliminary Issue. For this to be the case, proof of a route for unobstructed passage would be required.

In response, the defendants asserted that the right had only existed before 1702 up to the foot of Sutton mill dam. The river between the mouth and Sutton had always been tidal, and since in navigation law tidal waters are considered to be arms of sea, an undisputed right had always existed.

Upstream from Sutton was a different matter.

The 1702 Act proved a critical starting point in David Ainger's argument. Entitled "An Act for Making the River Derwent in York Navigable", with other clauses explaining that the river is "capable of being made navigable" and that … "The river may be made navigable", strongly suggested that the river was not at that time navigable throughout its length.

A further clue lay in a statement by the Petitioners for the Act from the Malton area, who in their supporting submission explained that they were at present "forced, at very great Charges, to carry and re-carry their goods many miles by land".

Other, older evidence also supported the limited extent of public navigation: on 13th May 1312 Orders, recorded in the Calendar of Letters Patent, were given by King Edward II, to block passage across, not along the Derwent, countering the contention that it might be used as an escape route; complaints in Mediaeval times about fish weirs blocking the Derwent were all, bar one, in the section below Sutton upon Derwent; a Charter of 1462 expressly gave powers to Conservators acting in the public interest, but these extended only as far upstream as the town of Sutton, and the Second Trinity House Report on the Aire and Calder Navigation of 1698 limited its scope over navigation to the next town from the mouth, probably Sutton, and certainly not the whole river.

Entries in the House of Commons journals for 15th January 1722, after the navigation had been completed, which had proved so valuable in understanding events at the time, also showed that complaints about charging for use of the formerly free waterway, related to downstream from Sutton.

A number of major obstacles in the river prior to 1702 also prevented through navigation. At the Domesday Survey by William the Conqueror in 1085 corn mills were recorded on the Derwent at several locations, such as at Old Malton, New Malton, Kirkham and Stamford Bridge. A mill at Buttercrambe in the 13th century is described in an Inquisition into the extent of the Lands there in 1292 when mention is made of a new mill dam here and the works done to it. Other mills worked alongside the Derwent at Howsham and Sutton; all would have needed dams strung across the river to function, blocking its course.

It was initially claimed in a primary piece of evidence, that the dams were constructed as part of the navigation, citing a map of works, including new locks round five mill dams, for making the river navigable produced by George Sorocold, engineer, in 1705.

The Plaintiffs were not alone in thinking that this is exactly what the map showed. Double parallel lines, clearly drawn lying within and across the river at various points

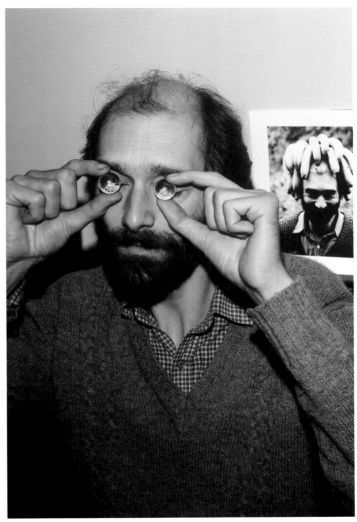

Left: *Omen spotter, Elaine Blake.* **Right:** *Chris Yates seeks to 'get in touch' with Izaak Walton for guidance over a difficult decision.*

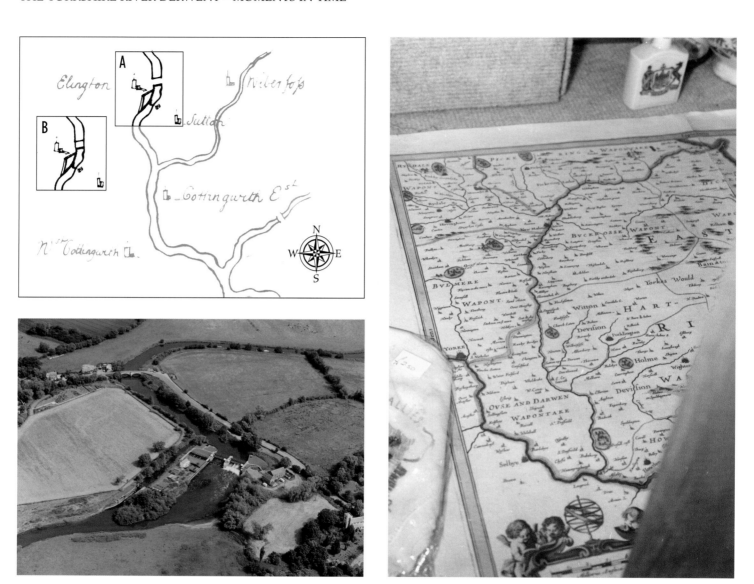

Top left: *Details of George Sorocold's 1705 engineering map of the Derwent Navigation, as originally drawn (A), and as traced over by conservers (B).* Bottom Left: *The same bridge today.* Right: *Janssen's map of 1654 provided the clues to identifying the meaning of the lines across the river on Sorocold's map.*

close to most of the proposed lock sites looked like locations for the building of dams to the defence team too.

Careful analysis of the highly detailed accounts for the making of the navigation recorded everything that was bought and the amounts people were paid. While there were entries for work carried out to the top of Sutton dam and the complete rebuilding of Kirkham dam, which had fallen down some twenty years before, there were none for the major constructions Sorocold's map seemed to suggest.

To begin with, it was not obvious that something might be wrong with the map. Until, one Sunday morning, walking past an antique shop in Malton, owned, coincidentally by one of the Malton Town councillors on the other side in the case, by sheer good fortune I spotted a framed copy of a map by Janssen, dated 1654, in the window. I took a photograph of it, went straight home, developed and printed the film, then compared the result with the version in the court papers. It was clear, either Sorocold had based his map on Janssen's, or that both had some common origin. Here lay the answer. Sorocold's lines were not dams to be constructed; they were existing bridges. Had he made a simple mistake, drawing the lines across inside the river banks, instead of over them? Later research was to prove it was not Sorocold's cartographic skills which were at fault.

Over the years, the original map had faded badly. To ensure its information was not lost, conservers at the Record Office had drawn over it under ultra-violet light to preserve the original lines, but tiny details had been misinterpreted. This subtle error would be confirmed from an unexpected source. In the records connected with the acquisition of the Navigation by the North Eastern Railway Managers in 1855, a tracing of Sorocold's map had been included. Produced when the original map was 130 years younger and less faded, the drawer clearly had a stronger image to work from. The details showed that Sorocold had originally drawn them correctly, as bridges, breaking across the river banks and that it was the over-tracing in recent times, which had changed their appearance and potentially their meaning in the case.

Exploration of the evidence in Court by David delved in forensic detail into the minute corners of the origins of the towpaths, the landing places, whether goods could have been loaded from bridge parapets, and who owned what; and that was before the judge started asking a series of probing questions.

Attention now turned to the Second Issue, the meaning of the 1702 Act. Paradoxically, the Plaintiffs sought to prove that the Act didn't create a public right of navigation past the Defendant's land. Whereas the Defendants argued that although it didn't expressly state it, it was obviously intended so to do; each side almost perversely arguing exactly the opposite to the ultimate outcome they wished to see.

It might have been convoluted, but it wasn't illogical. What mattered fundamentally to both parties was the effect of the 1935 River Derwent Navigation Revocation Order, which was equally silent about public rights, when it came to extinguishing the Statutory Navigation. Both sides agreed that the Order could only return the position to that which existed prior to 1702, unless any rights had arisen in the meantime.

Crucially, if the Act in 1702 hadn't legally created public rights of navigation upstream from Sutton, then the Plaintiffs argued that by long-user from the 1720s to the 20th Century, a public right would have been established – the Third Preliminary Issue. And they claimed that since the 1935 Revocation Order didn't expressly extinguish any public rights, an acquired right would have remained, unaffected, in place.

While a specific Act of Parliament created the statutory navigation, it was an Order under an Act – The Land Drainage Act 1930 - which revoked it in 1935.

Following severe floods in the early part of 20th Century a Royal Commission on Land Drainage in England and Wales reported to Parliament in December 1927. Part of the report explored the problem of derelict navigations, which were a nuisance to land drainage. Section 41 of the resultant 1930 Land Drainage Act dealt with provisions for extinguishing them.

In 1932, The River Ouse (Yorks) Catchment Board began the long process of making an application to revoke the River Derwent Act of 1702. Preparatory work for the Order centred on determining the extent of public rights of navigation, before the Act was passed.

It was the Defendant's view that the 1935 Revocation Order, the focus of the Fourth Preliminary Issue, simply returned the position to that which pre-existed the completion of the navigation in the early 1700s. It didn't need to expressly extinguish any public rights, as other than in the lower tidal reaches below Sutton, where there was no dispute, there were none prior to 1702; lawyers acting for the Ministry of Agriculture in 1935 had come to this conclusion too.

The Fifth and final Preliminary Issue, centred on the 1932 Rights of Way Act, commonly associated with the claiming of public footpaths and bridleways through 20 year-user, in which a footnote explained that, "for the purpose of section 8 of the Act, the term "land" shall include "land covered with water".

The Plaintiffs sought to interpret the footnote as meaning that the beds of rivers and lakes were covered by the Act and thus provided a mechanism by which rights of navigation could be claimed in the same way as footpaths and bridleways

The Defendants, for their part argued that, in the absence of any reference to rivers, lakes or navigation in the Act, its Memorandum, or during its progress through parliament, its purpose was to take account of fords, causeways and temporarily flooded land, not rivers and lakes.

During the case, a visit to the river was planned. In the midst of a severe thunderstorm, a comprehensive tour of numerous locations along the river took place. The judge, representatives of the Plaintiffs and defendants and legal secretaries, worked their way down the banks of the river in torrential rain, exploring the reality behind the long, sometimes esoteric arguments in which the barristers had been intensely engaged.

Next day, back in the formal surroundings of the Royal Courts of Justice, further questioning resumed. In Yorkshire, the support team would see only the tip of the iceberg of David Ainger's extensive analysis of the river and its history. But, setting up base-camp Butterwick was about to pay off.

Stephen telephoned: "In the absence of express mention of a full right of use for the public, the judge wants to know our justification as to why the Navigation was not intended simply for commercial use. Ainger needs an answer by tomorrow".

We were initially dumb-struck. How, almost three hundred years later, could we deal with that? This was an early Act of Parliament, with very little detail. But a response had to be made. I sat, staring out of the office window looking at the east end of Butterwick Church for about two hours, in search of inspiration.

Then it struck me. Below Sutton, the tidal river was an open public navigation for all uses before 1702. The Act embraced that stretch too, treating the river both tidal and non-tidal from its mouth as far as Malton as a whole. Logic demanded, in the absence of anything restricting the use below Sutton solely to commercial activity, that the status, which had applied here before the Act must have been envisaged to continue and apply to the rest of the river covered by the new Navigation as well. Otherwise, complaints that rights in the lower reaches were being diminished by the Act would have certainly followed. Back to London went the answer. It was a relief to have come up with one. Even more importantly the Judge seemed to think it made sense too.

More followed. Next the loading of boats from bridges and mills, including, in particular, a point about Menethorpe Mill needed to be addressed.

"That's not on the river" I explained to Stephen. The following day I walked up the centre of Menethorpe Beck with Tim Dixon. Tucked tightly into a small wooded area, the stream still cascaded though the barely recognisable remains of the old mill-race. This was the confirmation Stephen wanted; the mill was not directly on the river but half a mile up a side stream.

Next, the Judge sought proof that boats hadn't customarily worked upstream of Sutton in each pound between mill-dams to Malton prior to 1702.

Creation of the new navigation required the laying out of a towpath, or haling-way as it was known, along which vessels would be drawn by horses or by people on foot. Commissioners appointed to assess compensation for the riparian owners affected determined the amount to be paid, to whom and exactly where and what for.

Analysis of the schedule of land required and trees to be cut down to clear the bank edge for towing, transcribed onto a map of the river, was illuminating. While many trees had to be removed above Sutton, only one willow had to be cut downstream. This seemed at least to offer some evidence of the pre-existing limits of use; no trees, which would have snagged hauling ropes where vessels were working, plenty of them where the statutory navigation had yet to come.

The Plaintiffs countered, asserting that bank-side trees would not grow in the saline conditions of the lower tidal reaches, hence the reason for their absence, so it proved nothing. In reply, photographs of willows growing near Reed's Island in the River Humber with their feet in the water of the main tidal stream, were submitted to conclusively prove the point.

Debate about the origins and meanings of a Latin text from 16th Century Estate records of the Manor of Catton stimulated exchanges in Latin between the judge and both barristers, which left all others utterly dumbfounded. The lack of any consensus on the meaning resulted in a further challenging request. With only a typed transcript to hand, a copy of the original had to be obtained. There were 36 hours in which to respond; it would be a tall order indeed.

Humberside County Record Office held a version of the documents on microfilm, but obtaining a copy quickly could not be achieved. Breaking our self-imposed rule of never mentioning the case, we had no option than to explain to the archivist the purpose and urgent need. As suspected, anything to do with a court case, only made matters worse. Another way had to be found.

If copies of the copies couldn't be obtained, then maybe access to the originals, which lay in the archives at Petworth House in West Sussex, might be arranged. Ian Kibble would get in touch with the owners, Egremont Estates, while arrangements for someone to go to photograph them would be made. After two hours of intense phone calls an ambitious, precisely timed, plan had been devised.

At 6.00am the following morning, Joan Burnett took Tim Dixon to Leeds airport for a flight to London. At Heathrow a car had been ordered. Two hours later in Petworth House, the beautifully illustrated volume lay open at the very page. With photographs taken, a hasty drive back to Heathrow for the two o'clock plane, and a further hour later saw Tim back in Leeds. The negatives were processed, driven to the Clarkson's house, near Malton, to be printed, and while still wet, taken on to Chris Webb's house in York, for translation. It was way beyond good fortune that Chris could not only translate the mediaeval Latin, but that he could also read the document at all in the first place. Written in Court Hand, the script appeared wholly unintelligible to all but the specialist few.

Next morning, copies of the original documents, along with transcriptions, were on a train to Kings Cross, bound for the court.

After three weeks in the pressure-cooker of the High Court in the Strand the trial was over. But, there would be no immediate ruling. Not surprisingly, the judgment was reserved. All we could do was to wait, keeping our fingers crossed. David Ainger had argued the labyrinthine interpretations of the historic evidence, the 1702 Act, the 1935 Order and the 1932 Rights of way Act points, comprehensively presenting the matters of fact and law. We felt our evidence was compelling, but would the judge agree?

Overleaf: *Dawn over Malton from the Vale of Pickering on the 20th December 1989.*

CHAPTER TEN

Highs and Lows

*A roller-coaster ride of success, failure and nervous anticipation leads
to a national test-case hearing in the House of Lords*

A few days before Chritmas 1989, the call to the delivery of the River Derwent Navigation Case Judgment arrived.

The benches in Court were uncomfortable. All eyes were glued on the Judge. No one stirred. His speech was long and with the conclusions buried deep into the text, each took an eternity to unfold.

Working carefully in reasoned steps, Mr Justice Vinelott determined that: (1) there was no public right of navigation past the land of the Defendants prior to 1702; (2) that the 1702 Act did create a right for the public to use the navigation, subject, to the payment of tolls for cargo carried; (3) by virtue of the answer to the second issue no independent public right of navigation arose between 1702 and 1935; (4) that the 1935 Revocation Order returned the rights of navigation to the position prior to 1702; and vitally (5) the 1932 Rights of Way Act and subsequent Highways Acts legislation did not apply to rivers and lakes so as to be capable of creating public rights of navigation.

The Defendants had been successful on all of the Preliminary Points. But it would not be the end of the case; the Plaintiffs immediately announced their intention to Appeal.

At that moment, none of us cared much about what was to come. We were simply grateful for the result. That night,

back in the same room in Stephen's house in York where we had gloomily reviewed the evidence five years before, the team met up. This time, the mood was completely different. We toasted David Ainger and contemplated the messages we would give to the media the following day.

At home in Butterwick, the next morning I awoke early, got up and refined the press statements, before walking down to the end of the garden for some fresh air.

It was very cold and frosty as I wandered towards the old field pond.

An outrageous dawn was breaking. I am sure if I could have listened hard enough I might have heard the Halleluiah chorus. Just before I reached the pond something moved. In the grass lay a large fox, its rufous coat strongly coloured against the white rime. It stood up, but didn't run, only ambled slowly ahead of me to stop by the water's edge.

I paused, not wishing to disturb the fox further, turned and walked slowly back to the house. It was then that the full impact of the memorable events of the day before started to sink in. Thousands of people had backed the campaign, giving financial and moral support at every turn. It was a great comfort to know that the team had delivered the outcome they had hoped for, and that all of the campaign's supporters would be pleased with what they would be about to hear and read. At eight o'clock the phone started ringing.

19 December 1989: outside the Royal Courts of Justice.
From left to right: *Joan Burnet, Ian Kibble, Tim Dixon, Paul Smith, the Author, Stephen Warburton.*

Left: *De-stressing – Paul Smith, at Aldby Park with his son's galleon prior to a hearing.*
Right: *James Alexander Derwent Smith is introduced to his namesake.*

It was the press.

The result would be particularly important personally for Paul Smith too.

The following year, when Carole, Paul's wife gave birth to a son, in line with lawyer's tradition of naming a first-born after a memorable court case, his name had been partly preordained. As the Registrar repeated – James Alexander Derwent Smith, he hesitated at Derwent – what sort of name is that he enquired – "its a river" Paul explained. The Registrar shrugged his shoulders.

July 1991 saw the case back in court, this time before the Court of Appeal. We fielded the same team and planned the backup in exactly the same way as for the previous trial. It was a strong bench, comprising Lords Justices Slade, Bingham and Balcombe. With no Appeal lodged over the interpretation of pre-existing public rights before 1702, argument centred on re-examination of the remaining four points.

Again the weather turned blisteringly hot, on occasions, wigs came off, and again Paul was not happy; he still didn't like it when Judges felt it too uncomfortable to keep their wigs on.

Ten days later the repeat trial was complete. Again the Judgment was reserved. Again anxious weeks followed before the call to return to the Court. Can you be lucky twice we asked? Tension had reached breaking point. Regrettably the answer was No. On the first three Issues before the Court, the Judges agreed with Mr Justice Vinelott, but on the final and vital point for the Derwent and rivers and lakes throughout England and Wales involving the Rights of Way Act, they unanimously found that the trial judge was wrong, and that 'land covered with water' provided a perfect description of a river and lake.

When asked to grant leave to appeal to the House of Lords, the Judges refused. Equally worrying, the formula for the award of costs, which the Defendants would have to pay, seemed perverse and disproportionate to elements of the case on which they had failed. I carried out rapid calcula-

tions of the funding implications. We simply had to gain leave to appeal.

Having guided us faultlessly down the long road to the Court of Appeal, extra legal support for David would be needed if we were to try to proceed. We all welcomed the prospect of the extra energy a fresh mind would bring.

Fundraising, as well as legal preparations also had to hit top gear. A campaign forecast at the outset to cost £35,000, now teetered on the brink of a potential £600,000 bill.

Conrad Dehn QC, with whom David had worked on early opinions about the case, accepted instructions to take the lead. Under a strict timetable, a submission to the Appeals Committee of the House of Lords for Leave to Appeal – a sort of mini-judgement on the merit of allowing the appeal to go forward – was granted.

In October 1991 the final stage of the Case came before five Law Lords in the House of Lords.

This time Stephen and I based ourselves at the World Wide Fund For Nature's flat in London. With matters of interpretation of the law being considered, only visits to the Public Records Office at Kew and The House of Lords Library might be needed. By staying in London, we could reach both archives and respond quickly with ease.

At the conclusion of the hearing, Judgment was again reserved. Three months later, "We're on!", the terse message from Paul conveyed. This time, after the adverse costs issue at the Court of Appeal, he was determined to ensure that nothing went wrong. Boldly, he took the initiative by writing to suggest wording as to costs should the case go in our favour. On the day before the ruling, Paul contacted the Judicial Office of the House of Lords. Pressing the officer to inquire whether there would be a separate hearing on costs, should we lose, he was informed that there was no need. The Costs Order had already been included in the judgment.

We knew that for the costs to have been dealt with without further submissions, it could mean only one thing, that we had won. But we couldn't be sure.

Aldby Park, Buttercrambe, river, bridge and house, the possible site of King Edwin's 7th Century palace.

Overleaf: *Paul Smith hurries from the Houses of Parliament clutching an envelope, the contents of which will influence the future for the River Derwent and many other rivers in England and Wales.*

CHAPTER ELEVEN

A River Defined

After 7 years of legal submissions, argument and debate the
Ruling of five Law Lords establishes the meaning of a river.

Lawyers always work to instructions. On Thursday, December 5 1991, those agreed with Paul Smith were very specific and unusually formal.

Paul had been told to go into the Judicial Office of the House of Lords at 10.30am, pick up the two printed copies of their Lordships' judgment that had been ordered and to return to the pavement outside the Palace of Westminster where he would be met by Tim Dixon and me. Unusually Stephen had decided not to come, he simply couldn't face the tension in case the decision went the wrong way. Paul had also been told on no account to look inside the envelopes nor talk to anyone. It was important that he didn't know the outcome until we were ready and in the right place.

Court hearings, especially when it comes to the final results, are very tense times, and a few diversions to bring a smile or keep spirits up are a welcome relief to lawyers and clients alike.

To make a distinction between lawyers and clients in this case, would be to misrepresent the way everyone had cooperated. From the outset we had worked together seamlessly over research, public relations, fund raising, legal framing of information and management of the inter-related tactics to reach, or more correctly survive the pressure to get to this stage.

Throughout the long-running action, we maintained morale by retaining a sense of humour and laughing, not only at the ridiculous, but also at ourselves. On this momentous day I was determined to keep up our tradition by living-out the principles of a well-known legal adage, even at the expense of winding up the pressure, but Paul was unaware of what we were going to do. All he knew was that he must play fair and not look at the judgment.

The final issue at stake revolved around whether or not the Rights of Way and Highways Acts, normally associated with creating public rights of way on land, for example footpaths and bridleways, apply to water in a way, which can lead to claims for public rights of navigation. From the Defendants' point of view challenging this point wasn't about taking rights away from the public, merely about maintaining the status quo.

For 60 years, since the first of the Acts in question came into force, the general opinion had been that they did not apply to navigation. That is until summer 1990, when the three judges sitting in the Court of Appeal ruled that they did. In consequence hundreds of rivers throughout England and Wales were instantly placed at risks for claims for rights of navigation and the possibility of pressure for 'opening up' and associated development and disturbance which could follow. Such a scale of potential change would have implications for rivers and their wildlife in many places.

To make matters worse and unusually for English law, the Acts operated retrospectively. In the absence of appropriate actions as prescribed by the legislation it would be too late to protect rivers where there was now a risk. Few, if any, riparian owners had taken the necessary steps simply because they never for one moment dreamed that acts involving footpaths on land also applied to water.

Landowning, farming, angling and wildlife organisations all agreed that a hitherto important test case point had become a serious national issue. Now, six weeks after the October hearing before the five Law Lords, the moment of truth approached. Tackling a unanimous ruling, when all three judges in a strong Court of Appeal, had found against us was, everybody admitted, a Herculean task for Dehn and Ainger. We were fully prepared for the worst. Even if the ruling did go against us, we knew our supporters would have wanted to see the matter taken as far as we could. We hurried across Parliament Square to a bus stop in Parliament Street near the end of Whitehall. It was miserably grey, one of those days in mid-winter when it barely gets light.

The bus to Clapham took 15 agonising minutes to arrive. In the meantime, no one wanted to hold the envelope. We could hardly speak and conversation of any meaning or consequence finally deserted us.

"Here it is!." Tim announced.

Upstairs we were alone. Nothing seemed to exist beyond the limit of the steamed-up bus windows and the envelope. A few talismans collected during the course of the case, a pair of child's sun glasses, the otter skull and a lucky pot of River Derwent water were arranged on the seat beside us for good luck along with Alexander's woolly-hat, which Paul put on his head.

"Three to Clapham". "That's one pound each" and the whir of tickets coiling from the conductor's machine came the response. At last Paul could receive 'further instructions'.

"Okay, now!" my voice quavered.

Paul fumbled the papers out of the envelope, flicking and skipping in search of the result. Back and forth he went, looking intently for the conclusion to each of the Law Lord's speeches and whether the others agreed or not.

Minutes passed before he was sure what he was reading. Slowly, quietly and understated, he announced "We've won … it's unanimous … it's 5-0 … it's a lawyer's dream come true" – as if he really couldn't believe what he was saying.

Ironically, a few moments later the bus crossed the Thames. The main point in the case centred on the meaning of those four seemingly innocuous, but much debated words "in this Act …. Land includes *land covered with water*". The Court of Appeal had said that this was a perfect description of a river. Their Lordships did not agree, and obviously thought not even a lawyer would call it that. To support his view, Lord Oliver called on a literary extract to emphasise the point to good effect: "I cannot for instance think that any reader of Alfred Lord Tennyson would have regarded the Lady of Shalott, as she floated down to Camelot through the noises of the night, as exercising a right of way over the subjacent soil."

More directly they concluded that if the Act had been meant to apply to rivers and lakes and navigation it would have said so. But they were never mentioned.

Indeed, as we crossed the Thames we mused that it was again safe simply to call it a river. Paul explained that the ruling had done much more than that. For the first time in a thousand years a river has been legally defined. This was clearly important to a lawyer, but I felt we'd only been told something we and every other ordinary person on the top deck of the Clapham Omnibus already thought we knew – the best description of a river is a river.

But work still had to be done, including preparation for the formal ruling in the House of Lords and communicating the results to supporters, as well as at a media press conference later in the afternoon. But we stayed on the bus all the way to Clapham, walked to the Common, then took a cab back to Paul's London Office. Two versions of a press release had been prepared, measured responses to cater for

Tense Times. Left: *Waiting for the Clapham Omnibus near Whitehall.* Top right: *Paul Smith, on the top deck heading for Westminster Bridge, about to read the historic Law Lords' judgment.* Bottom left: *Paul Smith, Tim Dixon (wearing Alexander's lucky woolly hat) and the author (with lucky pot of water and otter's skull) at Clapham Common.*

A river relieved from the uncertainty of change.

success or failure, though we now already knew for certain only one would be needed.

At 2.00pm barristers for both sides, one of the Defendants David Brotherton, Paul, Tim and myself gathered on the floor of the otherwise empty House of Lords. Looking much smaller than on television, brightly coloured and sparkling, intricate and ornate, a sort of cross between a heavily gilt religious shrine, a mediaeval panelled house and a sumptuous leather furniture showroom, it was awe inspiring.

Their Lordships sat on a bench to the right. Lord Bridge rose to conduct proceedings. Paul explained that a cost-efficiency, job-sharing exercise was taking place. Firstly Lord Bridge stood in for the Lord Chancellor on the Woolsack (a sack full of wool) formally explaining why they were there. He then hopped across a few feet and turned round to look at where he had been standing, speaking this time for himself, but talking to the empty space where he had been substituting for the Lord Chancellor, as if in a Parliamentary debate.

Others of the Law Lords spoke and agreed. The judgment ended with the award of all costs to the Defendants.

Back at the Solicitor's office, the rest of the Team and our main supporters were phoned. First to be called was Anne Henson, one of the most closely involved Defendants, along with Roger Preston another of the people against whom claims were served   Out riding, Anne was overwhelmed with joy and relief at the news. Carol Hatton at the World Wide Fund For Nature, the largest single backer of the campaign, gasped in excitement and disbelief. Then we contacted Stephen, followed by David Bird, Allen Edwards and Bruno Broughton, stalwart contacts with anglers throughout the Campaign, and of course Izaak Walton, 'through' Chris Yates. At that moment a dream for some, really had come true.

Curiously, the House of Lords, though the highest 'court' in the land is a part of Parliament, rather than a court of law. Any ruling therefore has to be registered as a legal judgment back in the High Court.

One other major step remained. The framing of the overall Order of Discontinuance of any further action and the apportionment of costs.

In a private hearing in Chambers, back in the High Court, the precise wording to finalise the Case was agreed. Even at this stage, Stephen continued to note everything down with undimmed enthusiasm. Negotiations over the final costs settlement were on a knife-edge. Outside the court door I debated a solution with the Plaintiffs' representatives, with Paul pressing me to conclude a deal before the judge got to the end of the hearing. But a number of things simply had to be in place. Finally, with minutes to spare, at last a package was framed, comprising transfer of property and an agreed sum of money. It was a compromise, with which probably neither side were one hundred percent happy. But maybe that's the essence of a good compromise, a conclusion in which no one walks away feeling they have got everything they want. A line had been drawn. It needed to be.

Overleaf: *Purchase of Ellerton Ings helped save Ellerton church as well as acting as a springboard to many other conservation projects.*

CHAPTER TWELVE
The Ripple Effect

Out of the Derwent Court Case grew a web of direct action for conservation, spreading both locally and far from the River.

After initial success in the High Court in 1989, the River Derwent Appeal Group awarded me an honorarium in recognition of the work that had been carried out. It struck me that setting up a charity to reflect the Group's aims would be the best use of the money. Stephen and Jan could be the other trustees. When it was suggested by the solicitors that it might be called the Carstairs Countryside Trust (CCT), I didn't give the name a second thought; I never imagined the trust would have a public role. How wrong I would be. If I had realised the extent of what was to come it would never have been given such a personal title.

Not long after the Charity was registered, The Nature Conservancy Council (NCC) approached CCT with a request for it to act swiftly to buy a meadow at Ellerton, which was up for sale. They saw a need and the Trust had the mechanism, if not the money. The land comprised 24 acres of Ellerton Ings, a traditional hay meadow Site of Special Scientific Interest (SSSI), and the adjacent 20 acres of Ellerton Abbey Garth, the site of a 12th Century Gilbertine Priory and a Scheduled Monument (SM). Saying yes was the easy part; finding the funds at short notice another matter entirely.

Michael Woodhouse, Land Agent at the time for NCC in York, solved the problem. He suggested that he visit the National Heritage Memorial Fund (NHMF) in London to

brief officers Julia Burdett and Henrietta Ryott about CCT, its potential role and the importance of the acquisition. Established in 1980 as a lasting memorial to those who have given their lives for the United Kingdom, the NHMF acts as a fund of last resort for heritage acquisitions of national importance. Michael did a good job. Within a few weeks the support of the NHMF had been secured, along with substantial help from the World Wide Fund For Nature, English Heritage and NCC, as well as the Burton and Mitchell Charitable trusts.

Traditionally farmed, Ellerton Ings was in good condition. Ellerton Abbey Garth, the site of the Priory was not. Until about 1980 the field had been a pasture, in which the old village cricket pitch sat in a levelled area among the humps and bumps of archaeological remains.

Like so many archaeological sites at that time, it was then bulldozed flat and the land ploughed annually for arable production. Halting the damage was the first task, followed by reseeding and reintroduction of low-intensity grazing.

With ownership, preliminary archaeological evaluation of the Scheduled Monument could take place. Local people remembered seeing tiles, bricks and wall structures when the land was ploughed. But little evidence could be detected from the ground. To gain a better view, we tried attaching a radio-controlled camera to a kite. But there were snags. A strong wind was needed to lift the assembly, so strong that the kite veered too quickly about the sky. And it simply couldn't legally fly high enough to gain a full vertical view of the 20 acre field.

Professional aerial photographs were needed. Neil Mitchell, from Beverley, had developed an economically efficient way of providing them, by grouping clients' work together. He was also well disposed to helping the trust.

One of his contracts covered photographing the progress of a construction site in North Lincolnshire. His monthly route from the home-base airfield, near Thirsk, took him directly over Ellerton. Each time he passed, vertical shots of the site would be taken, to establish if any crop marks from the buried archaeology could be seen.

Crop marks are mysterious and ephemeral things. There would be variations in colour and texture and patterns of mowing of thistles, but after nearly a year, still no evidence of the archaeology could be identified. Neil kept trying.

In early September 1990, following an extremely dry August, everything suddenly changed. Torrential rain stimulated a flush of new grass growth. With differentials in the soil characteristics, grass grew first over the damper parts such as filled in ditches, revealing across the site in a brighter green, the pattern of the monastic settlement. Once the growth over the rest of the field caught up, the fleeting pattern soon disappeared.

Guided by the images, geophysical surveys of the prime area where buildings had stood were commissioned. Two techniques were used. The first employed a magnetometer which detects variations in the magnetic characteristic of the soil and the degree of influence by human activity, in comparison with the natural background levels of the earth's magnetic field. The data are collected by walking up and down lines a metre apart taking readings at regular intervals. The second, utilising a resistivity meter, involved walking to a similar grid pattern, but this time taking readings of the variation in the strength of an electric current passing between two prongs pressed into the ground; the greater the

dampness in the soil, the higher the value of the reading.

When combined in a computer, the results of the research confirmed in greater detail the structure of the archaeology buried beneath the field.

Soon after CCT acquired the Ellerton Abbey Garth, news filtered through of a proposal to demolish the adjacent and unused Ellerton Church.

Many redundant churches are sold for alternative uses. But such a course of action had failed at Ellerton, due to the building being land-locked between the surrounding field and an active graveyard. Consequently, adequate access could not be provided to attract a potential buyer by the Church Commissioners; a situation made progressively worse as the years passed, by the building's deteriorating condition.

It might have been late in the day, with gaping holes in the roof and windows smashed, but with acquisition of the surrounding land by CCT, access problems could be resolved and perhaps the building saved.

With a few days to go, the proposal to demolish was put on hold and negotiations opened to transfer the old church into a new trust, to be formed especially for the task. But, it would be some while before the funds to restore it could be raised and the transfer of ownership completed.

In its early years, CCT acquired further parcels of meadowland along the Derwent floodplain and beside the old Pocklington Canal. By now, an 'Approved Body' under the Wildlife and Countryside Act and the third largest landowner in the Ings, trustees designated most of its holdings in the Lower Derwent as a part of the National Nature Reserve. Of the purchases, those at Thorganby and West Cottingwith gave perhaps the greatest pleasure, when after four hundred and fifty years, CCT reunited in ownership land owned by the Gilbertine Priory, with the site of the Priory in Ellerton. During preparatory research for grant applications to pay for the land, historic records showed that in Mediaeval times a local person held part of the land for life on payment of a root of ginger. Looking in the Oxford English Dictionary for the

Marking time. **Top left:** *Stone-carver, Peter Maris, prepares a boundary stone for the Carstairs Countryside Trust.*
Bottom left: *Farmers, Len and Stuart Charlesworth invent equipment for their tractor for moving the half-ton stone.*
Right: *Jan Knowlson, then Chairman of CCT and James Goodhart, a supporter, celebrate setting the stone in position.*

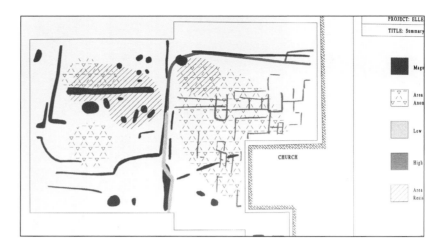

Top left: *An aerial photograph of Ellerton Abbey Garth reveals the crop marks caused by buried archaeology.* Top right: *Resistivity and magnetometer readings are combined and interpreted to create an impression of the pattern of the buried archaeology.* Bottom left: *Taking magnetometer readings across the site of the Priory.* Bottom centre: *Jan Knowlson, Chairman of CCT, hands a root of ginger to Nicholas Woolley (plus a cheque) in exchange for the deeds of West Cottingwith Ings.* Bottom right: *Undergrounding overhead electricity supply lines across the Ings.*

word 'Ginger', it turned out to be only the third known use of the word in the English language.

Ownership of West Cottingwith Ings opened the door to solving another long-running Derwent problem. Between East Cottingwith and Thorganby, overhead electricity cables stretched across the Derwent Valley. At about thirty feet high, they formed a lethal 'cheese-wire' for inflicting harm on the 50,000 plus birds passing across them twice a day in winter. Estimating the number and species of birds killed was not straightforward; they would either fall into the floods, or be eaten by foxes, which had learned to patrol under the line. But one thing was certain, the landscape and the birds would both be better off without them. Agreement from Yorkshire Electricity to underground a mile of the line, supported by an exceptional grant from the Heritage Lottery Fund (HLF), saw the cable 'moled' through the silts under the river from East Cottingwith to Thorganby in one of the fastest pieces of unobstructed work the contractors had experienced.

Other CCT projects involving the Centre for Wetland Archaeology at the University of Hull led to the Centre carrying out a cored transect of buried river silts across the Derwent Valley and Ellerton Ings to establish the historic development of the river and its floodplain after the Ice Age. Alongside the data gathered for the river, research also indicated that the pollen samples in the bed of the supposed fish pond in Ellerton Abbey Garth were almost 100% cannabis; hemp-retting, not fish production seems to have been its primary historic use.

Founding CCT had been carried out almost on a whim. It was an organisation of the type to be able to act swiftly, in the right place at the right time, with many links to the right people. But none of its achievements would have been possible without the grants provided by a range of national and local organisations and charitable bodies. And as far as saving Ellerton Church was concerned none could have been more significant than the HLF. For the church it came in the nick of time.

The ripples flowing from the Court Case had already travelled a very long way.

In addition to CCT's work in the Lower Derwent, and with changes in trustees to involve Joy Allan, Ian Kibble and Stephen Greenfield, major sites for wildlife, archaeology and the palaeoenvironment have been acquired and managed for conservation, spreading from near Doncaster, to Scarborough, Northallerton and the coast.

Other groups have been encouraged by CCT's experiences, with trustees assisting in the development of further conservation trusts in Barnsley, Cumbria, Peterborough, the North York Moors, Ripon, Doncaster and Sykehouse.

And the ripples would run and continue to run a lot further still.

Above: *Barn Owl.*
Overleaf: *The redundant Priory Church of St Mary and St Lawrence, Ellerton, after restoration by the specially-established Ellerton Church Preservation Trust.*

CHAPTER THIRTEEN

Sense of Place

A redundant Victorian Church and Parish Maps reflect local pride.

"Queen of the Ings": no one could disagree with this apt description of the beautifully positioned Priory Church of St Mary and St Lawrence, Ellerton, standing isolated above the 13th Century monastic Abbey Garth and the sweep of the Derwent's floodplain.

But, redundancy as a working church in 1978 left its prospects looking grim. Fifteen years later, agreement by the Church Commissioners to transfer ownership into a special Preservation Trust, changed all that. Heralding in a new era for this symbolic building, it also brought a focus around which the community would join with the trustees, led by Phil Thomas, to drive forward an imaginative restoration scheme.

Negotiating to take possession of a derelict Grade II Historic Listed Building, at the same time as raising the money to carry out the extensive works to the fabric followed an intricate process. Numerous steps, ranging through Canon Law and Faculties, culminated in the passing of a Pastoral Measure to take account of the new opportunity, and freeing the way to transfer ownership of the building. But ownership without the resources to carry out the repair work would have been folly; having the funds to do the work without ownership, pointless. Both had to be brought forward together.

The launch of the National Lottery in 1994 couldn't have been more timely. Of equal importance, the cooperation of conservation architect Peter Pace, to produce a costed feasibility study for restoration of the building, addressed a fundamental step. Without their support, today instead of an inspiring building, its place in the landscape secured into the immediate future, we would be facing an empty space, lamenting the loss of the most tangible expression of the community rooted back hundreds of years. A local resident succinctly described the prospect of its demolition as - "like losing the full stop to the sentence that is the village".

Preparing a Lottery bid was by no means simple. But if large sums of money are involved it's not unreasonable that applicants should have to work a little in return. Apart from anything, the process of carrying out background research and planning the project is both an education and a discipline which stands organisers in good stead. A point proved during background research, through the discovery of the original architect's specifications during visits to Hull University and Lambeth Palace libraries. As well as descriptions of the materials to be used, they showed that the Victorian structure had been rebuilt from an earlier church.

The present Ellerton Priory Church, an early example of the work of the esteemed Victorian architect, John Loughborough Pearson, completed in 1848, stands on the site of its mediaeval predecessor, pulled down as unsafe in 1845. While new materials were brought in for its construction, the scheme re-used much of the earlier stone work, maintaining a link, albeit in a reorganised form with the 13th Century Gilbertine Priory, dissolved by Henry VIII in 1538.

The Gilbertines, founded by Gilbert of Sempringham, Lincolnshire, about 1130 comprised the only English monastic order. Unfortunately, with all of the Order's written records lost or destroyed, only the remains of their buildings and sites, such as at St Mary's Church, Old Malton, upstream on the River Derwent and at Ellerton Abbey Garth, offer an insight into their way of life.

With the award of a grant from the Heritage Lottery Fund (HLF), the Ellerton Church Preservation Trust took possession of the building and plans for restoration could be put in place.

It is testimony to the HLF's sensitivity to the church's location, lying as it does at the end of a narrow road through the village, that proposals for use as a quiet space and for special events, in keeping with the spirit of its history and setting, were readily agreed.

Significant work lay ahead for the Trust. The roof had caved in at one end and most of the windows were smashed. Water leaking from gutters and obstructed by long-failed drainpipes and drainage channels exacerbated the situation. With scaffolding erected and closer inspection of the upper walls possible, the extent of the problems grew. Like many building restoration projects, until access can be gained to the higher levels, the true extent of the task cannot be accurately assessed.

Firstly, the building needed to be stabilised, cleared out and made safe and secure. Even this was not straightforward. When human use ceased, with windows now broken and a roof gaping to the sky, avian occupants moved in; an ideal place to call home for pigeons, and an equally great abode if you are an owl.

Each night hundreds of pigeons returned to the church to roost. And for many years, barn owls had nested on top of a wall inside the ruinous nave. As a specially protected species, timetabling of work would be critical to avoid disturbing them during the breeding season.

An imaginative plan, developed with Tim Dixon, at the time the Nature Conservancy Council's site manager for The Lower Derwent Valley, would see the owls cleverly re-located into a new living space.

Peter Pace designed a barn owl entrance hole, in a style he believed Pearson, the church's Victorian architect, would have used, if he had been incorporating one at the time. Positioned in the gable above the east end of the nave, where it joins the chancel, it offered an elegant future front door for the owls. But encouraging them to downsize from a whole church to a rather smaller 3 foot square alternative home would take a deft multi-step manoeuvre.

A tarpaulin, battened down over the roof to prevent further deterioration of the fabric, closed off one avenue of access for the owls. With all of the broken windows, except at the east end, boarded up, a barn owl box, with an opening door in its rear, was added behind the new owl entrance, though with its 'back door' left firmly shut.

Prevented from using many of the previous openings, only a fly-way through the east window remained. Several days later, with the birds accustomed to this route and while they roosted inside, all remaining windows, bar the small top part of the east window, lying below, but in line with the nest box in an owl's-eye view, were also boarded up.

A further week later, with the owls now using the even narrower access, and with them inside, the last window was blocked and the door in the back of the nest box opened.

That night, the birds left to hunt for food through the back of the nest box and out through their brand new front door. While they hunted, Tim again climbed the long ladder high inside the building and shut the door on the back of the nest box, closing off their access to the inside of the church. It worked perfectly. When the owls returned, their space had significantly reduced in size. Nevertheless, the next spring, the pair bred successfully in their new if rather restricted home. However, in later years they would face some stiff competition from Jackdaws for this prime

The Revd. Christopher Simmons,
blessing the new cross on the Priory Church of
St Mary and St Lawrence, 23 April 1998.

"To the Glory of God, the builder, Jesus Christ
the Corner Stone and the Holy Spirit, inspiration
of all craftsmanship and beauty, we dedicate this
cross, that all who see it may be reminded of God's
love for the world and in his name we ask a
blessing on all who work for the restoration of
this building, that through their dedication and
skill it be once more a sign of the eternal in the heart
of the community, for Jesus Christ's sake, Amen"

Top left: *Inside Ellerton Church before restoration works begin.*
Top centre: *Patrick Wildgust dumps another barrow-load*
of pigeon guano cleared from the church.
Top right: Phil Thomas *(above), Chairman of ECPT and*
Peter Pace, architect, inspect the high level works.
Bottom: *The Revd. Chris Simmons dedicates the*
new cross with a prayer.

avian residential location.

Clearing the mess from inside the church, a combination of collapsed lime render, pieces of roof and slates and more than a decade's worth of pigeon droppings along with quite a collection of their last mortal remains, posed an unpleasant task.

Following public meetings in Ellerton, work parties supported by villagers embarked on removing the debris and improving the site in readiness for the start of restoration works. Farmers came with tractors and trailers, other residents with shovels, spades, shears and wheel barrows to clear away scrub, remove trees and improve drainage at the base of the walls, as well as to cart scores of barrow loads of guano from the church floor.

During the clear up, one of the villagers made a startling discovery by the south wall of the church, near to the porch. Cutting through grass to clear along the base of the wall he hit something hard. The obstruction stretched for several feet. Carefully removing the turf, buried just below the surface he exposed the clearly inscribed grave stone of Johannis de Wyntringham, Canonicus, a small cross in a corner, indicating his connection with the historic Priory. Later research in York Minster library confirmed his role there during the 15th Century.

Washed with clean water to enhance the contrast, in the flat light the ancient inscription looked almost as sharp as when it was first carved.

Early stages of renovation of the church brought more problems, when close inspection of the bell-turret led to a nasty surprise.

From the ground, the stonework appeared sound; close too it was clear that a century and a half of scouring wind, blasting from the west across the Ings and whipping up and round inside the top of the turret, had stripped away the backs of the stones to barely an inch thick in places. Iron staples and ties, binding the stonework had corroded and expanded, bursting joints. Nothing held the loose assemblage of stones that was the turret together and

in place, except for good luck, gravity and perhaps divine intervention. There was no choice, the turret had to be dismantled and rebuilt, significantly increasing the cost.

By the time of the 150th anniversary of the consecration of Pearson's church, a new gilded simple cross graced its rebuilt bell-turret, glistening against the sky.

On a bright and sunny afternoon, the Reverend Chris Simmons joined Stephen Warburton and myself on the scaffolding at the top. Revd. Simmons brought with him two things, a special prayer he had written, with which to dedicate the cross, and a bottle of home-brew beer to pour over the top of the turret and to toast a key moment in the story of the building.

It was a wonderful feeling to be high up, like sitting in the top of a tree as a child but better, with an unparalleled view over the Abbey Garth towards an un-seasonally large flood along the Ings. It was a place to contemplate for a moment the world of the monastery and the pattern of life which had unfolded below us over the years.

Amusingly, we were not alone. We noticed a troupe of about two-dozen woodlice heading up the turret towards the cross. What had encouraged them to set off on their epic journey from below? Where did they think they were going and had they any idea of what they would do when they got there? We joked that if they could be posed the question "Why are you doing it", their answer in all probability would have been an all too human "because it is there!"

Three days later, on Sunday the 26th April at 3.00pm, the exact time of the original consecration 150 years before, Phil addressed a large group of local people, visitors and well wishers from the steps of the Queen of the Ings - 'A Phoenix, rising from the ashes' that the church had become. Cocooned in a web of scaffolding, the encouraging backdrop of a building coming back to life, framed Phil as he enthralled the guests with his legendary exposition and architectural tour.

Progress with restoration continued at a measured pace. The tumbled churchyard wall has been rebuilt, roof and windows replaced and restored, walls re-pointed, church furniture and fittings recovered and installed, walls re-rendered and decorated. A remarkable achievement of a few people, capped by national recognition by the award of the Council for the Protection of Rural England's Mark for 2005, for its contribution to the environment, and the creation of a new stained glass window, by Helen Whittaker, winner in a 2002 competition, supported by The Worshipful Company of Glaziers and Painters of Stained Glass. In a tapestry of translucent colour, Helen's intricate design unites the wildlife, the agriculture and religious occupation of the site in a deep sense of place. An unloved and uncared for building, set in a landscape of immense cultural importance has been gradually taken back into the hearts of local people.

A small but telling confirmation of the importance of the building is to be found in the Ellerton Parish map produced in 1997.

The Derwent Parish Maps project, inspired by a national initiative of the organisation Common Ground, and run by English Nature, encouraged communities along the river and its tributaries to creatively identify features within their parishes which they valued and to record them artistically in the form of a map - a local heritage mini modern Domesday. Maps in different media were created by 18 communities linking from East Ayton and Helmsley in the north, to Wressle in the south. Information on the Ellerton and Aughton Parish map emphasises the importance of the churches to the character of both communities, with each building marking the western end of the settlements close to the Ings. The details for Ellerton lead with the description of the church and the work party, which discovered the grave stone of Johannis de Wyntringham, as well as other memorial stones from the past.

Its writers could not have foreseen that just a few years later another poignant memorial would be set in the church nave's north wall. Beautifully designed, it remembers Stephen Warburton, who in 2004 died of cancer in York. His memorial stands for all to see in a place he cared deeply about, in sight of the meadows and in earshot of where the call of the wildfowl carries across the water through the night on the winter's winds.

The new East Window of the former Priory Church of St Mary and St Lawrence, Ellerton, designed and created by Helen Whittaker.

Overleaf: *Ellerton Ings.*

CHAPTER FOURTEEN

Coal Comfort

When workings in the Selby Coalfield reach the river, threats from subsidence bring a ground-breaking agreement with industry to look after the Derwent's meadows and birds.

Coal mining is coming. That was the message when a Withdrawal of Support Notice, posted in 1994, informed owners of land in North Duffield, Ellerton, Aughton and Bubwith that subsidence could affect their properties at any time.

Hearts sank. A new wave of potential problems faced the Derwent's meadows. With very shallow gradients across the Ings, even slight changes to their levels or drainage patterns could have significant effects on the species composition of the protected grasslands and the feeding conditions for wildfowl and wading birds.

The issue of the notice under the terms of The Coal Act, a final step before mining begins, enables landowners to review their property so its condition can be compared with any changes which might happen, and to take preventative measures if anything dangerous could occur. Subsequently, where there is economic loss, or structural damage, compensation can be claimed. Quite separately, the Nature Conservancy Council (NCC) would ensure that protection of the statutory nature conservation value of the land would be taken into account.

None of this should really have come as a surprise. But concentration on the Navigation Court Action meant that local conservation eyes had been focussed elsewhere for many years. The Notice was merely the latest in a succession of similar steps, which had crept across the local landscape since 1976, following the Secretary of State's Approval for mining for coal from the Barnsley Seam in the Selby Coalfield, the largest coal mine in Europe at the time.

In the Lower Derwent Valley, the eastern limit of the mining consent followed the boundary between North Yorkshire and North Humberside (formerly a part of the old East Riding of Yorkshire) from near Elvington to Breighton.

Mirroring the administrative boundary, the agreed limits of the consent, while largely following the centre line of the river, deviated to either side in a number of places, such as at Bank Island and Wheldrake Ings.

However, a special condition, known as Condition 2 for short, meant that mining could not take place nearer to the river than half the depth of the seam, ie about 1700 feet, without consulting with the River Authority over the flood banks and the NCC over the Ings.

Fifteen years after consent for coal extraction, with its galleries, tunnels and massive underground cutting machines, working reached the vicinity of the river. In 1990 British Coal in line with the requirements of Condition 2, applied to the Mineral Planning Authority (North Yorkshire County Council) to be allowed to work up to the centreline of the River Derwent from under North Duffield Carrs, the name given to the Ings here and one of the original areas designated as a Site of Special Scientific Interest in 1975.

Under the terms of the 1976 planning consent NCC had no legal scope to object, only to seek appropriate remedies if any harm occurred.

Agreement reached with the NCC to mitigate the effects of the predicted subsidence, required a series of ditches, bunds and pumps to be installed around the Carrs to manage the resultant increase in wetness. The pumps would also provide a means to manage water levels for nature conservation. Ironically the very land, which had been the focus of so much energy to oppose agricultural pump-drainage in the early 1980s, for totally different and unavoidable reasons, had water levels managed by pumps after all. Though now NCC would control the levels for dedicated conservation benefit, instead of the Internal Drainage Board solely for agricultural production.

By 1994, extraction of coal from under the Carrs neared completion. It was the proposals for further working, envisaged just to the north and opposite Ellerton Ings, which led to the notice of withdrawal of support.

The Trustees of The Carstairs Countryside Trust (CCT) were perplexed at the prospect of the Trust's land at Ellerton being subsided from the effects of mining crossing the river. The land fell outside the original planning consent boundary and searches of the local authority's records when it had been acquired made no mention of a consent, which would result in such an effect.

NCC staff entered into extensive discussions with RJB Mining (UK) (RJB), the mine operators. Tim Dixon, the National Nature Reserve Site Manager argued forcibly that any mitigation works for subsidence, must, as at North Duffield Carrs, be carried out before the new mining work commenced. Equally forcefully, Chris Bennett, for RJB, expressed the opposite view, that the Company's consent allowed mitigation to be addressed afterwards, if harm occurred.

A complex situation was destined to become even more difficult. Simultaneously, with the application to extend mining, the European Union Habitats Directive, enshrined in the UK Habitats Regulations 1994 required Planning Authorities to review all active planning consents where there might be conflict with environmental considerations on designated sites, such as the Derwent Ings. If harm to the special interest of the site was likely to occur, action to remedy it had to be taken. But before that could happen, the further extension of mining to the centre line of the river, forced on by commercial imperatives underground, needed to be resolved, before the Review could be completed.

Environmental consultant Neil Humphries, engaged by RJB, predicted no harm would occur. But a precautionary approach had to be taken. Eventually, after months of negotiations an acceptable solution was found. A worse case scenario plan identified the maximum area which might be affected of the rare MG4 grassland habitat, for which the Ings are famed, as well as elements of bird habitat, and then multiplied it by 5 to account for any difficulties.

Financial computations then arrived at a figure of almost £300.000, which would be deposited by RJB for compensatory land acquisition based on the grossed-up area of land, experimental MG4 grassland re-creation, management works and on-going monitoring of any impacts from subsidence on Ellerton Ings.

Importantly, the funds would be paid into a new trust, The Last Great Wetlands Trust (LGWT), to be run by independent trustees, who would administer the money and oversee implementation of the plans. Receipt of the funds fulfilled RJB's obligations, bringing clarity to the position and freeing the way for mining to proceed. As it turned out, monitoring after the mining had taken place would show, exactly as Neil Humphries predicted, that no harm had occurred; a massive bonus to conservation around the Ings had been indirectly and unexpectedly achieved.

With a solution to the Condition 2 area working in place, review of the overall consent under the Habitats

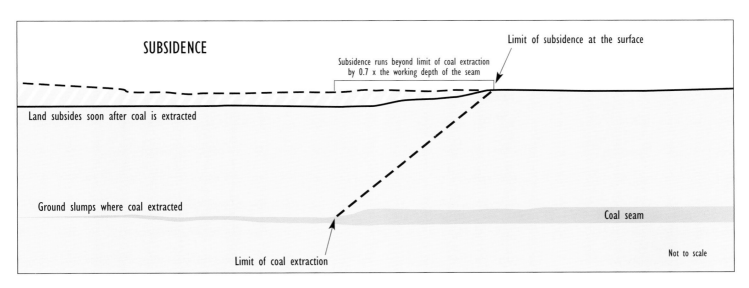

SUBSIDENCE

Limit of subsidence at the surface

Subsidence runs beyond limit of coal extraction
by 0.7 x the working depth of the seam

Land subsides soon after coal is extracted

Ground slumps where coal extracted

Coal seam

Not to scale

Limit of coal extraction

Top: *The diagram explains how subsidence runs beyond the limits of mine workings.* Bottom left: *An aerial photograph of Ellerton Ings shows the area to where subsidence was predicted to reach.* Bottom right: *Stephen Warburton and Jan Knowlson demonstrate how shallow the residual flood is and the land's vulnerability to changes in levels making it deeper.*

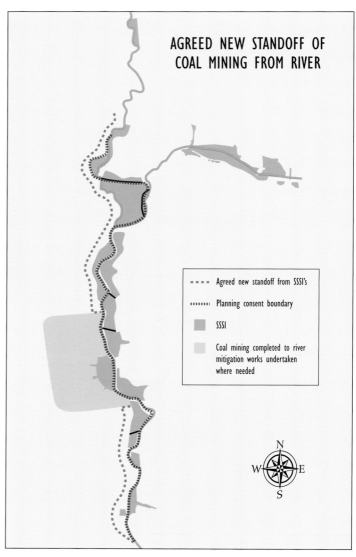

Above: *Looking northwards over a high flood in West and East Cottingwith Ings and Wheldrake Ings. The flooded areas delineate the international wildlife sites, all of which were removed from risk by RJB Mining's agreement to draw back the planning consent boundary of its coal mine.*

Right: *A diagramatic plan of the agreement with RJB Mining to voluntarily move back the coal-working line.*

Regulations, which had been progressing in parallel, could also move towards a conclusion.

If the Derwent Court Case had seemed complicated, unravelling the needs and obligations of the interrelationship connected with the mining planning consent and the environmental requirements of European and national legislation, ran it a very close second, only a lot less fun.

Newspaper headlines, responding to public concerns about the future of the Ings, simplistically and wrongly reduced the whole matter to "Jobs versus Birds". We knew it didn't have to be that way; there could be jobs and birds, but that doesn't sell newspapers. Apart from which, what politician would put 400 people out of work if there existed a way to avoid it?

For some two years, from the introduction of the need to review the consent, nature conservation interests, notably the World Wide Fund For Nature (WWFN), The Yorkshire Wildlife Trust (YWT), the Royal Society for the Protection of Birds (RSPB), the Conservation Society of the Yorkshire Derwent (CONSYDER) and the Carstairs Countryside Trust (CCT) had been encouraging North Yorkshire County Council (NYCC) to undertake and complete the task, but little progress had been made. The Council, the statutory regulator, EN and the mine operator, RJB had reached stalemate, caught in a seemingly unresolvable vicious circle.

Coalmine plans change constantly in response to operating conditions and geological factors. Since the mining company did not know exactly where working would lead, predicting the effects on habitats and wildlife into the future was impossible. And if you couldn't predict what would happen, the Review couldn't be carried out.

Fortuitously, CCT's land ownership at Ellerton, which had already paved the away to save Ellerton Church, now proved pivotal to helping EN, NYCC and RJB Mining to conclude the Review of the Selby Coalfield Planning consent. Ownership of land, both here and elsewhere on the Derwent gave CCT, with the YWT, a clear position to participate in the

issue. It suited everyone that CCT's trustees, free from wider organisational constraints, should take the lead.

Initially, mounting a legal challenge to the Withdrawal of Support Notice had been discussed by conservation bodies. This was soon dismissed when, after an appointment to inspect the plans, it emerged that predicted subsidence lay between zero and one inch across Ellerton Ings. It didn't take a genius to work out that no one would contemplate going to law over such a small amount. It might matter critically to a golden plover, but we couldn't see much public or political sympathy for such a course of action, in the face of placing people's jobs at risk, especially since scientific research already predicted that nothing would actually be harmed.

To begin with, a number of landowners in Ellerton Ings, including CCT, had refused access to the mine company for habitat research as part of their application to mine to the river from under North Duffield Carrs.

In the light of the predicted subsidence data and the political reality, all agreed to work together, allowing research to ensure the data were as comprehensive as possible for the County Council and EN to consider.

Confrontation had changed to cooperation. It wasn't that anyone had conceded anything, only that common sense dictated that there might be a better way of handling the situation than adopting polarised positions and arguing through the press.

Having familiarised ourselves with the mine plans, a meeting was arranged with Bill Rowell, Managing Director of Deep Mines and Chris Bennett, his Operations Manager, who agreed to explore the wider position with the regard to the stalemate over the Planning Consent Review.

Encouraged by RJB's responses, Carol Hatton (WWFN), Tim Dixon (EN), Stephen Warburton, wearing his YWT hat, Ian Kibble (Country Landowners Association) and I met with Bill and Chris at Kellingley Colliery

The bottom line centred on the fact that the potential for mining could affect almost all of the Ings.

I asked Bill the simplest and most obvious question to resolve the issue. "If everyone supported you, would the company be prepared to pull its line back voluntarily"? Come back in six months and I'll let you know, he replied. At least the answer wasn't NO.

In six months I called Bill. He invited me to another meeting. This time, only Ian Kibble accompanied me. The company seemed amenable to finding a way forward; I agreed to act as honest broker between the main parties, promising that if a formula could be found, it would have the support of all the major conservation organisations as well. EN and NYCC agreed to the novel approach.

Six months of intense shuttle diplomacy followed, grinding through ideas. Gradually a workable formula emerged which didn't require extensive and impossible research.

It comprised an arrangement, known as a section 106 agreement, between RJB, NYCC, EN, CCT and YWT.

In the Agreement the area of the Ings covered by the planning consent would be split into three – north to south (see map page 120). In the northern and southern sections RJB would voluntarily restrict its working to a new stand-off point half the working depth of the seam back from the western boundary of the Sites of Special Scientific Interest, instead of from the river, which lay beyond.

Further it was agreed that if the company wished to work under the area between the new line and the SSSI boundary it would have to apply to NYCC, whereupon, only the area which might be affected by subsidence would be reviewed. If there were shown to be risk of harm, this could then either be mitigated for or the company could then claim compensation for not being able to proceed.

In the central section, provisions had already been made through the deposit of funds, for mitigation for any risk of harm as part of the application under Condition 2, though no actual harm was envisaged.

Finally, the agreement committed YWT, CCT and EN to allow the company's consultants access to their respective lands for scientific research if the need arose. It was extremely hard and tortuous work, thinking a way through the problem, but in the end the outcome by any reasonable standards resulted in an unqualified success.

Without prejudice was removed, confidentiality lifted and the news announced in the press.

Sadly, some people didn't trust the result and comments tipped press coverage from positive to negative views. It was their prerogative to express how they felt. But we were all deeply disappointed that the edge had been taken off a spectacular groundbreaking agreement and RJB and its staff denied the congratulations they deserved. However, it did serve to confirm that the decision to resolve the issue, initially behind closed doors, was right.

Complaints to the Local Government Ombudsman, that NYCC had been deficient in its procedures and timeliness, were lodged by the objectors. The Ombudsman did not agree with their views, comprehensively endorsing the value of what had been achieved.

Looking towards All Saints' Church, Aughton from the banks of the River Derwent.
Subsidence from coal workings in the vicinity of North Duffield would marginally affect Aughton Ings too.
Overleaf: MG4 grassland.

MG4 stands for 'Mesotrophic Grassland Type 4' as described in the botanist's bible for the description of plant communities in Britain – the National Vegetation Classification. Mesotrophic means neutral, and this type of grassland is typically found on the rich neutral alluvial soils along lowland river floodplains. Historically these grasslands would have been the most valuable parts of village agriculture, providing lush and rich hay-crops, and ample aftermath grazing for cattle and sheep, and would have been constantly re-fertilised by the annual deposition of silts at times of winter flood. Their antiquity and continuity of management have resulted in a dazzling array or community of wildflowers characterised by the abundance of great burnet and meadow foxtail, but also including a wide variety of other plants. In most areas of the country, these fertile lands were the first to be ploughed for more intensive agriculture when incentives were available, and coupled with the embankment of many rivers for flood prevention purposes which prevents the deposit of silt, this has resulted in the demise of this special grassland community. The Lower Derwent is now one of the prime locations of 'MG4' left in Britain.

CHAPTER FIFTEEN

Sowing Seeds

Major funding from a mine company underpins a trust to monitor meadows,
buy land and to experiment with the re-creation of rare grassland.

Establishing the principle of creating the Last Great Wetlands Trust (LGWT) to administer the funds deposited by RJB Mining (RJB), as part of its planning consent to work coal in the vicinity of the River Derwent, took only a half an hour. Turning it into a reality, took nearly two years.

Two vesting trustees, Tim Dixon and myself, appointed by English Nature (EN) and RJB, brought the trust into being. We enlisted nominees for permanent trustees from EN and RJB, as well as seeking other individuals with connections to the Local Authority, farming, nature conservation and the community. With permanent trustees in place, we stood down, though I would subsequently be invited back to take on the role of Chairman.

With a full complement of trustees in place, addressing the Trust's roles and responsibilities began.

All did not run smoothly in the early days. Campaigners, set against the coal mining, challenged the trust's role, involving local MPs and the Minister for the Environment. Trustees were resolute that they had taken on a very specific job. It was not their responsibility to debate the merits of that role, nor to satisfy other demands.

When an issue arose over the Trust's name, resulting in a request from EN national staff to change it, trustees were more than a little bemused. They never understood why the request was made, but clearly something, somewhere lay behind the approach.

But, nothing hung on the name, though it was quite a nice one, suggested by EN in the first place. Although a little irritated at having our strings pulled from elsewhere, the change was agreed. Alternatives included the Stan Barnsley Conservation Trust, named after the two coal seams, Stanley Main and Barnsley. But on reflection it sounded too close to the industry for a conservation trust.

In the end, The Lightowler Trust was chosen. It was a little joke really, in the face of the mild irritation at being asked to change the name and the repetitive and persistent letters about the trust from campaigners, officials and politicians.

During the River Derwent Court case, documents discovered told of a man called Lightowler, living at Elvington Lock, who poached eels from the waters of the neighbouring estate. This had been happening regularly for a very long time. In the archives, respectful letters complaining about his activity from the aggrieved Estate's agent to his counterpart, showed enduring restraint. Then, after perhaps twenty years, patience ran out. "Lightowler, he's at it again. For God's sake let there be an end to this!" the agent exploded. "Let there be an end to this" struck a chord. Lightowler Trust it would be. Only it didn't stay quite that way. A secretary at the solicitors, bewildered why a conservation trust would be called Lightowler, assumed it must be two words and split it. So Light Owler, it became.

The first task for the Trust involved acquiring land to mitigate for any potential harm from mining subsidence in the Ings. Whether or not harm actually happened was irrelevant, the funds were there and the trustees agreed that the project should start straight away with the meadow recreation experiment. If harm did happen, the experiment would be in place, and if it didn't there would be a benefit anyway.

Matching land of low fertility with the required area and in the right location was never going to be easy. That which did come on the market proved mostly unsuitable, for one reason or another, or the owners inexplicably on two occasions withdrew after an offer had been made.

When 68 acres, twice as much as required, at South Grange Farm was identified by Tim Dixon, purchase was pursued. The land comprised about 30 acres low fertility grassland, exactly the area needed, with the rest farmed as arable fields.

With the land's suitability for the experiments confirmed by Neil Humhries, completion of the purchase gave trustees the land they sought. Following preparation of a business plan through Neville Turton, then of Carter Jonas and later to become the Trust's land agent in his own right, initial land management works began.

Importantly, the arable land, which was surplus to requirement for the experiments, was retained as a working endowment rather than sold. Not only did it provide an added inducement for a tenant to farm the land, but also a buffer for the grasslands and opportunities for further beneficial conservation work.

Nest boxes for barn owls were erected, hedges brought back into good condition and a location as part of the re-introduction programme for the rapidly declining grey partridge was established.

Among the first steps required to bring the land into good order, a new wider gateway to access the land from the Howden to Sutton upon Derwent road had to be formed. Crossing the highway boundary into the field needed planning consent. Following an application to the East Riding of Yorkshire Council, a fusillade of objections arrived, some certainly rude and others bordering on defamatory.

Objectors predicted that following the application for a gateway, one for a coal mine would be lodged. Somebody was fuelling a campaign of disinformation. We could have professed and argued our position, but it was pointless. No one seemed to want to listen. The problem lay in that the field sat in line with the place where some years before, a withdrawn application for mine access tunnels under the river had been made.

On scientific matters, environmental consultant Neil Humphries, assessed the characteristics of the land in detail and produced a project plan to experiment with the re-creation of MG4 grassland. Based on the principle of trial strips, with the help of farmer William Ward, the land would be ploughed and disked, and green hay cut from the nearby Ings of Len Charlesworth, would be spread evenly over its surface. Using green hay prevents loss of seed heads, which are allowed to ripen after cutting and spreading. Control strips, which received no hay were left for comparison.

Weather and the timing of the experimental works played havoc with trying to get reliable data in the first few years, but in due course a dramatic result appeared. Tiny plants of species such as pepper saxifrage, great burnet and narrow-leaved water-dropwort, along with grasses, such as meadow foxtail, meadow barley, creeping bent and red fescue, all components of the MG4 grassland on the Ings sprouted and grew. In parts, plants of yellow-rattle, which helpfully suppress the growth of aggressive grasses also germinated successfully.

Trustees were delighted. The time had come to invite others to share in the experience. Organised as part of the twenty-fifth anniversary celebration of the founding of the

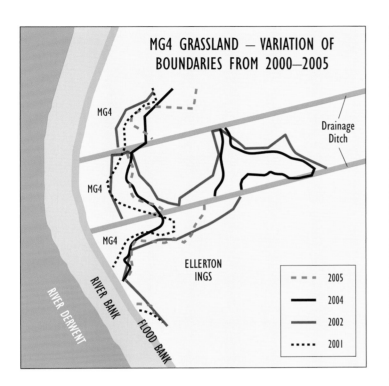

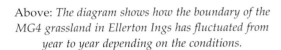

Above: *The diagram shows how the boundary of the MG4 grassland in Ellerton Ings has fluctuated from year to year depending on the conditions.*

Right: *MG4 grassland is found on the shallowly sloping ground above the residual level of the water once the initial flood has subsided. The aerial photograph shows the same area as depicted in the diagram.*

National Heritage Memorial Fund, The Light Owler Trust, joined with The Lower Derwent Conservation Society (LDCS), The Ellerton Church Preservation Trust (ECPT), Carstairs Countryside Trust (CCT), English Heritage (EH) and EN to jointly celebrate their work.

On a glorious summer day in July 2005, with curlews flying overhead, Jeff Lunn explained to guests the progress of the experiments before a visit was made to Ellerton Church to see the restoration work carried out there and a most agreeable afternoon tea, courtesy of Deirdre Falcon from the LDCS Group in Ellerton village.

The other main task facing the trustees of the Light Owler Trust involved monitoring the land at Ellerton Ings to detect any impacts from mining on the rare grasslands. Each year Neil Humphries, assisted by his colleague Paul Benyon, assessed the limits of the MG4 grassland in Ellerton Ings, comparing them with the control area further south in North Duffield Ings.

Financial plans allowed for twenty years of annual monitoring, even though subsidence occurs soon after mining ceases. After three years no detectable harm was observed. Neil advised that further monitoring would be a waste of time and money, freeing substantial funds for wider conservation work connected with the Derwent.

Neil's advice made eminent sense, although periodic monitoring in the Ings would be continued to learn more about the dynamics of the Derwent's floodplain and the management of the grasslands.

Incredibly rare both nationally and locally, MG4 grassland grows on the shallow gradient of the land just above the floodline, with soil characteristics, nutrient levels and dampness playing inter-related parts in its distribution. Although the combination of plants characteristic of MG4 can tolerate inundation for long periods in winter, once the growing season begins, any remaining standing water is a serious matter.

Erratic weather, maybe fuelled by climate change, now had a substantial part to play in the direction of further research. Following un-seasonally and long-lasting late floods along the Ings in 2003, the MG4 grasslands had been significantly reduced. Seeing an opportunity to add greatly to knowledge, additional research addressed two further factors. It needed to confirm clearly that changes were due to the weather and not to the effects of mining. It then aimed to assess the way in which the grassland would respond when conditions returned to a more normal pattern.

Within two years we had a conclusion. Reassuringly MG4 in the riverside fields could readily re-establish itself, in some places extending further than the area it had occupied before. The diagrams, drawn from the research shown on page 127, illustrate the changes from year to year.

With research patterns established and positive results from trial strips on the Trust's land at South Grange Farm achieved, attention turned to conducting a large-scale field trial at the farm. Effects of erratic weather again influenced the results of the experiment when frequent torrential rain rendered the test area underwater for much of early 2006, badly suppressing growth. But this is early days and this is the reality of conducting experiments. Unexpectedly, the best results in the trial strips happened when things didn't work out as planned. Similarly, the suppression of the growth over the larger area may obscure equally surprising results in the future.

To capitalise on conservation benefits, with the Trust's ownership of the arable land at South Grange Farm, a new initiative to help threatened plants of arable fields, many with interesting and attractive names such as shepherd's-needle, hen-bit dead-nettle and weasel's-snout, is being considered. Working with the Trust's tenants, the Wake family two acres will be sprayed to remove unwanted vegetation, ploughed, disked and left to assess the plants which spontaneously appear, before utilising the land as a site to safeguard arable wild plant species grown from local seed.

South Grange Farm with fenced-off trial areas used for the MG4 grassland recreation experiment.

Overleaf: Winter on CCT's flood meadows at Low Catton.

CHAPTER SIXTEEN

Handing on the Baton

The Derwent's worth, fully recognised, is carried into the future through high-tech research and management.

Three days before Christmas 1995, another bombshell hit the Lower Derwent Valley, when Yorkshire Water (YW) submitted an application to the Department of the Environment, for an Emergency Drought Order to allow increased abstraction from the river. After threats from pumps, boats, bank side developments and coal mining, now more water could be sucked away too.

It fills most reasonable people with suspicion when Statutory Authorities and other major organisations announce plans for significant issues with short consultation periods spanning a holiday period. It might have ruined a few Christmases, but after years of battling for the Derwent, local conservationists were not about to be defeated by such a move.

Undeniably, the water industry had problems. After severe droughts across the Country during 1995, over large areas of England demands for water were barely being met. But compromising the Derwent as an easy solution brought a firm response.

Robust objections were marshalled and submitted over the Christmas break. English Nature (EN), then filed an uncompromising and unequivocal objection that it would "not consent". Selby District Council did likewise citing "the potential impact on a site of international nature conservation importance" and perceptively, "the absence of a detailed evaluation of the environmental and hydrologi-cal implications", the basis on which to develop a new approach to the problem would soon be found.

Yorkshire Water postponed the proposed hearing of its Drought Order submission and eventually the application was withdrawn. Perhaps they saw the writing on the wall and rather than lose, sought an alternative way forward, or maybe it rained enough. But a tide was turning. The message that disregarding the Derwent's environmental value would be at one's peril, had begun to sink in

Seizing the moment, Jeff Lunn, then Manager for EN in York, proposed a solution. Why should the parties involved not work together to assess ways of achieving sustainable management of the water resource, integrating it with the environmental needs of the River and the Ings. YW agreed, the Lower Derwent Project was born and the future management of the Valley entered the field of concentrated research, high science and voluminous reports.

A three-way partnership between YW, EN and the Environment Agency (EA), co-ordinated by Liz Chalk, the EA's Projects Specialist, was established, later to be joined by the three Internal Drainage Boards covering the critical area.

From the outset the partners addressed the wide-ranging concerns about the Valley and its water resources by focussing on one clear aim "to achieve the sustainable management of the water resources of the Lower Derwent Valley".

Not long into the Project, the issue of the Barmby Tidal Barrage reared its head again. Several Ings farmers, the Yorkshire Wildife Trust (YWT) and the World Wide Fund For Nature (WWFN), believed that the Barrage may be having an adverse impact on the haymeadows of the Ings and might not be adequately considered.

With the notification of the River Derwent as a European Union Special Area of Conservation (SAC), activity affecting it now fell within the scope of the Regulations.

The farmers and their supporting organisations argued that the operation of the Barrage is a 'Plan or Project' within the meaning of the Habitats Regulation and that like the Planning Consent for the Selby Coalfield it should be reviewed. However, the EA did not accept that the particular part of the Regulations cited applied to the operation of the Barrage.

Backed by YWT and WWFN, the farmers sought a Judicial Review in the High Court of the EA's position. But the applicants withdrew the Judicial Review proceedings having received a written undertaking from the EA that it would review the operation of the Barrage and its effects on the Ings and make modifications if necessary.

While no final conclusion had been reached on the relevance of the European Regulations to the issue, after nearly thirty years, scrutiny of the Barrage's operation had been placed firmly onto the agenda.

Under the Lower Derwent Project five principal issues would be assessed. These comprised: poor drainage of meadows at times of high river flows, especially involving the operation of the Barrage; the condition of the flood banks, and the potential of flood defences to reduce the deposition of silt which naturally provided nutrients for the floodplain grasslands. Other matters involved water quality issues and the impact of bank-side tree cover on fisheries and navigation.

Phase One of the Project concentrated on increasing understanding of how the water and ecological processes work within the Valley. The investigators then sought to explore the relationship between the processes, so that the impact of abstractions could be reviewed. The consequential increase in science-based knowledge would then help in the formulation of water and land management decisions which might need to be undertaken.

Based on the information gained, Phase Two examined the relationship between the ecological character of the individual Ings within the floodplain and the factors which influence them.

Exhaustive research involved collating existing information as well as detailed new surveys and the addressing of wide ranging hydrological, hydrodynamic and water quality considerations, through computer modelling.

An ecological 'model' based on indicator species and habitats known to be associated with particular water regimes in the valley provided a means to assess the present status and to project potential effects.

Weighing up the data, ecological indicators for both the river and the grasslands were identified.

Across the floodplain, analysis of the meadows presented a complicated picture, with thirty different types of grassland, fen and swamp vegetation plant communities, governed by gradient, wetness and nutrient levels. The intricacy of different grassland types is well demonstrated in the map shown on page 133 depicting their distribution in Bubwith Ings. And analysis of the range of birds and their favoured locations categorised the Ings into different sectors, depending on the nature and level of use by the birds.

A number of the principal issues to emerge resulted in a series of management actions being put in place. Potential losses of sea and river lamprey, which migrate into the river to breed, due to the impact of barriers to migration such as weirs, inaccessibility of suitable habitats and entrapment on the abstraction intake screens of a number of abstractors provoked concern and the need for a response.

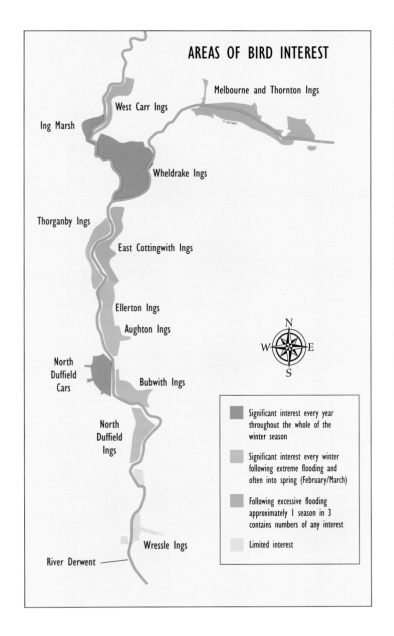

AREAS OF BIRD INTEREST

Melbourne and Thornton Ings

West Carr Ings

Ing Marsh

Wheldrake Ings

Thorganby Ings

East Cottingwith Ings

Ellerton Ings

Aughton Ings

North Duffield Cars

Bubwith Ings

North Duffield Ings

Wressle Ings

River Derwent

■	Significant interest every year throughout the whole of the winter season
■	Significant interest every winter following extreme flooding and often into spring (February/March)
■	Following excessive flooding approximately 1 season in 3 contains numbers of any interest
■	Limited interest

Floodplain

Vegetation

The flood meadows support a mosaic of over thirty d
and swamp vegetation communities (Fig.3 shows the
Bubwith Ings). The different vegetation types are rela
moisture, with reed sweet-grass swamp (National Veg
located at the wet end and meadow foxtail – great bu
Classification type MG4) located at the drier end of th

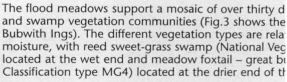

Great burnet

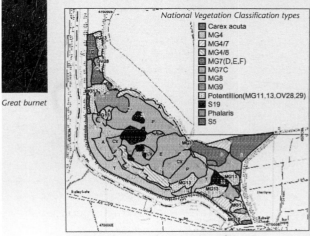

National Vegetation Classification types	
■	Carex acuta
■	MG4
■	MG4/7
■	MG4/8
■	MG7(D,E,F)
■	MG7C
■	MG8
■	MG9
■	Potentillion(MG11,13,OV28,29)
■	S19
■	Phalaris
■	S5

Fig. 3 Map to show the distribution of flood meadow vegetation at
Bubwith Ings in the Lower Derwent Valley 2002. © Crown Copyright.
All rights reserved. Environment Agency, 100026380, (2005)

Above: *A diagram of Bubwith Ings in the Lower Derwent Project
report identifies many different types of grassland vegetation,
some extremely rare and each given a special classification
reference number which are found here.*

Left: *The diagrammatic map identifies the various different Ings
areas, each of which needs its own special treatment to maintain their
wildlife interest, along with their relative significance for birds.*

Evaluation of the operation of the Barmby Barrage suggested that there is no evidence that it causes loss of MG4 grassland, which is still well represented in the valley, though when taken with other factors the possibility exists that it could have some impact in the future. On the other side of the coin, given the potential effects of climate change and sea-level rise, the Barrage might have a beneficial effect by restricting the level changes of progressively higher tides.

However local farmers are now worried that at times of low flows, loss of the scouring effect of the river, impeded by the barrage, is contributing to siltation at bank edges, affecting ditch levels and drainage outfalls and consequently the quality of the grasslands in the Ings.

To refine the operation of the Barrage, an upgrade to the computerised control system was put in place in 2003, together with monitoring to identify any additional river management required.

Critical to the condition in many of the Ings is the state of the drainage channels with one-way flap-valves at their outfalls into the river. These allow water to discharge, but prevent a rising river from flowing back into ditches.

Overall the Project found the valves to be in good condition, though several in the vicinity of Wheldrake Ings and East Cottingwith Ings required maintenance to remove silt and trapped debris on the river side of outfalls which affected their efficient operation.

In a collaborative effort, Natural England (NE), and The Internal Drainage Boards are fine-tuning the maintenance regimes to improve the biodiversity of the main drains, as well as working with individual farmers to optimise the maintenance of smaller drains and field ditches. In the Ings themselves, further work is also underway to investigate the impacts of field drainage and hay-cutting dates on the various vegetation communities.

In response to inappropriate levels of nutrients from Waste Water Treatment works, notably phosphorous, entering the river and influencing the Ings, nutrient removal schemes are being implemented by YW at Malton, Stamford Bridge, Seamer, Pocklington, Pickering and Melbourne. Initiatives to address more diffuse pollution entering the river system throughout the catchment are also being implemented.

Sympathetic tree management to reduce shading of the restricted habitats of aquatic plants, while maintaining habitats for otters and lampreys is being carried out. Surveys to monitor river depth, bed levels and siltation, which can clog gravel spawning grounds and habitats for aquatic plants are underway. To ameliorate the effects of sedimentation, attention is being focussed on reducing soil run-off, not only to protect the river, but agricultural land as well.

Improvements to fish passes at weirs on the river and at the Barmby Barrage to ease the passage of migratory fish to their potential spawning grounds are also being investigated.

Importantly, the studies identified the deleterious impact of disturbance on breeding and wintering birds, particularly by walkers, especially with dogs, on the river banks. At some sites evidence shows that in certain seasons birds are in the air 70 percent of the daylight hours as a result of this disturbance and that there is need to review the management of access to these places.

Publication of a Lower Derwent Management Plan for the period up to 2010, covering both the river and the Ings in individual detail, consolidated the findings of the research, bringing a firm and valuable conclusion to the Project. A dismal prospect three days before Christmas in 1995, had turned, ten years later, into a leading example of care for the countryside, demonstrating that with cooperation, major issues for the environment can be addressed without confrontation to the general benefit of all.

It also showed, exactly how challenging it becomes when natural systems, which once functioned in harmony with a traditional farming system, are knocked out of balance by sudden major change. Further it revealed the technical lengths we have to go to if we are to now maintain and protect the area into the future. Put simply, to protect a place we must understand it. And this is what it takes to gain that understanding. Without it our options and our confidence to pursue appropriate courses of action would be severely limited. Worse may well be to come, as the effects of possible climate change will add to the problem.

While attention focussed on the Lower Derwent, at the other end of the River a more modest scheme – The Upper Derwent Project - prompted by the increased appreciation of the Derwent's ecological value, responded directly to problems facing the river in its reaches above East Ayton.

Championed by the North York Moors National Park Authority, the programme, run by Kier Brown, was coordinated by a range of partners, from government bodies, to local councils, anglers and interested individuals. Using European Union funding, it sought to help protect and enhance the Upper Derwent catchment for its wildlife, social and economic value, through three courses of action.

Grant aid targeted at conservation, community and fishery work, acted as a catalyst for activity. Advice and training over river management, including assistance for farmers and landowners enabled them to obtain financial support through other environmental schemes such as Countryside Stewardship. The final prong of activity supported research into the dynamics of the river in these upper reaches, as well as establishing both the requirements and population size of key plants and animals which utilise the river system.

Between 1998 and 2001 more than 37 agreements were established to, among other things, manage bank side vegetation, which would allow increased light onto the river, survey riparian mammals, produce interpretation boards and leaflets about the Forge Valley National Nature Reserve and implement erosion control measures.

Prior to undertaking these works an audit of the geomorphology of the Upper Derwent catchment addressed the perceived issue of silt deposition problems in Forge Valley. The audit identified where the silt originated and what factors led to it being deposited. And the location of areas of high erosion were also established.

From the assessment, it emerged that low flow rates and a wide channel, rather than excessive silting were causing the problem. Unsustainable dredging to remove silt was discounted as a remedy. Instead, a range of different styles of weir were installed to control and vary the flow rate in different parts of the river. Diversity in the flow could keep gravel areas free from silting, while allowing silt to gather in less damaging places.

Species action plans were prepared for the white-clawed crayfish and the water vole, for which long term records of their presence in the Upper Derwent are known.

Surveys showed the crayfish to be present, sometimes in high and healthy numbers, throughout the catchment, though signs of the water vole were sparse. The presence of these and other important species such as otter, brown trout, grayling, bullhead, brook lamprey, kingfisher and dipper, served to highlight the value to the environment of the work undertaken by the project.

As with many aspects of life, the management of the Derwent is now embedded in a sophisticated array of scientific research and monitoring, far beyond what could have been imagined in the past.

With its importance widely accepted, in the last ten years The Lower Derwent has also fallen within the scope of the Humber Head Levels Land Management Initiative and its successor the Humberhead Levels and Moors Partnership, while the whole river and its catchment also lies within the embrace of the slightly curiously named SPROUT (Strategic Partnership for the River Ouse and its Tributaries) Project, established to satisfy one of the aims of the environment theme of the York and North Yorkshire Sub-Regional Investment Plan to 2009!

Comprising a partnership of twenty organisations the SPROUT Project has prepared an 'Opportunities Plan' covering regeneration of waterfronts, enhancing access and leisure activity, increasing wildlife, reducing flood risk, promotion of renewable energy sources and improving people's knowledge about how river systems work, though at the time of writing the precise plans have yet to appear.

All this is fine, in so far as it goes, as long as regeneration, enhancement and promotion do not stimulate new demands, expectations and uses beyond that which is appropriate, which organisers then feel obliged to accommodate to one degree or another in a bid to keep everyone happy.

In our present world of tick boxes, strategies and the ability to analyse everything to a high degree, these are the inevitable consequences of the way these things are now done. But, however necessary and valuable this work might be, it does seem a very long way away from the spirit of the days when the tide ebbed and flowed into the river, and from the natural order of things being played out along its quiet reaches, in the ditches and meadows as the procession of the seasons follow their annual cycle.

Within all of these initiatives, one ingredient is of paramount importance. If we look back, it wasn't plans and projects or organisations and research per se that have saved the day for conservation. It has been people, individually, or working the system with a clear aim in mind, who have pursued their own little corners of the cause with spectacular cumulative effect. The question is, who will pick up that baton for the future? For as long as there is something worth protecting, there will always be a job to be done.

It is an obvious thing to say, but the natural environment, modified as it might be, can and should be respected and valued for its own sake. It should also be protected for our own sanity. For we need there to be wilder places to counter the pressures of modern life and to recharge our souls.

No better emphasis could be placed on this and what it means on the Derwent, than the publication in 2005 of Craig Ralston's Historic Review of the Birds of the Lower Derwent between 1850 and 2002. Like Stephen Warburton's book thirty years before, Craig's Review is not just a catalogue of the past, but a testimony to the present and an inspiration to everyone who cares about the future. Leaving space for the natural world is a vital part of our quality of life, not a play-thing to be valued when it suits, then sidelined when it gets in the way of some other pursuit. If we subscribe to the principle that our best countryside should be looked after as a priority, then we should not compromise its well-being.

Craig's book provides a comprehensive perspective on the birds' comings and goings; offers a tribute to the efforts of those who record the birds throughout the seasons and the years, and shows how concerted efforts for conservation have enhanced the existing species present. It reminds us that this is still a lived in and working landscape, but one operating in a gentler way and at a slower pace than much of the rest of our modern world.

This tangible summary epitomises the enormous environmental quality of the Ings, while offering a sobering perspective on their vulnerability as an island of traditionally farmed land set in a wide sea of intensive agriculture and domestically occupied surroundings. It defines, just what a rare jewel this little-known part of the English countryside has become.

SPROUT, the latest umbrella project, unavoidably invites me to think of Brussels. This is no bad thing.

It cannot be over-stated, how important a part European legislation has played in ensuring that traditional farming of the Ings can be supported and that the Derwent's natural attributes have to be taken notice of by government.

I have little doubt that it is the influence of the European Union, coupled with inexhaustible local effort that have held the line long enough for the message that the Derwent is a clear Case for Conservation, to get through.

The Derwent Ings

Final Word

An Ever-rolling Stream.

When Craig Ralston released Wally the whimbrel into the night sky at 10 o'clock on 5th May 2005 the Derwent's story entered a new dimension.

Each year several hundred of Wally's 'mates', as Craig described them, roost at night in a remote and undisturbed part of the Lower Derwent Valley on their journeys between wintering grounds in West Africa and breeding grounds in the Sub-arctic, such as Iceland. During the day they rely on a handful of fields in very particular areas of the surrounding countryside in which to feed.

They have probably always done so for as long as whimbrels have passed this way, but their roost was only discovered in the 1980s.

Unknown to Wally as he disappeared into the darkness, except perhaps if he ever worked out what the tiny satellite tracking device attached to his back was all about, the world was watching his every movement.

Now the combined efforts and enthusiasm of local ornithologists Dave Tate, Steve Huddleston and Mike Jackson working with Craig and supported by a number of conservation organisations, would put Wally's wanderings firmly on the map. But it would do much more than that.

Capturing the imagination of people across the globe who logged on to follow Wally's progress on his own website, brought home the importance of the staging places, such as the Lower Derwent Valley, on which birds depend as they chart their time-honoured journeys.

Why were Craig and his colleagues doing this? They had a very good reason. Birds which depend on precise locations to 'refuel and recuperate' on long migrations are highly vulnerable to the loss of habitats. A classic and depressing example, the demise of the slender-billed curlew, a close relative of the whimbrel, graphically shows how a species can slip towards the oblivion of extinction when essential staging places are changed or destroyed.

Knowing where whimbrels feed locally and the places to which they travel, will help to protect their futures. And if their futures are secure, so too will be the landscapes and other wildlife which also rely on them.

To understand the significance of the Derwent to migrating birds, you need only to imagine the human equivalent. You are on an airliner from South America to Europe which traditionally refuels on the Azores in mid-Atlantic, only when you arrive the airport has been closed for good and the runway is no longer there.

In June 2006, somewhere in West Africa, Wally's tracking device fell silent. No-one will ever know why. Had he been eaten, had he been shot or trapped, had it fallen off and Wally flown on without it, retracing his annual journey?

But the message he had already sent was clear, emphasising the need to maintain and protect the Derwent Valley from change. And that involves people.

Like every drop of rain and stream feeding into the river, each person connected in any way with the recent history of the River Derwent has left an impression of one sort or another. All, like me will have their own unique stories to tell.

From anglers and angling clubs, naturalists and nature conservation organisations, landowners and farmers to navigation interests, councils and drainage boards, working together or disagreeing, each has played a part in the course of events resulting in today's spectacular scene.

But nothing and no-one exists in isolation. If there had been no CONSYDER and no court battles, difficult as they were for both sides at the time, many other wide-ranging conservation benefits would not have followed. The Carstairs Countryside Trust, its land acquisitions and other trusts it has since encouraged would not exist; Ellerton Church would in all probability have been demolished; no agreement over the Selby Coalfield would have been reached and hence no Light Owler Trust to follow.

The Derwent's story would have been completely different. It might have been better, it might have been worse. But this could be said for any part of the English countryside. There are no rights and wrongs, just opinions and actions and a resultant direction to the flow of events influenced by them all.

When the Yorkshire Naturalists' Trust bought Wheldrake Ings to protect its birds, life on the Derwent was rather simpler. The plants grew, the birds arrived and the farmers took the hay and livestock grazed the fields.

Now thirty five years later, wintering wildfowl arriving from the north, descend into a much more complicated world, their final approach through invisible layers of necessary bureaucratic regulations and projects.

Down through SPROUT, the Humberhead Levels and Moors Partnership and the Lower Derwent Project, come the geese and swans; down through the National Nature Reserve, they descend; down through the Ramsar Wetland of International Importance, the EU Special Area of Conservation; wigeon whistling on their final approach through the EU Special Protection area for Birds, and the most precious layer of them all the Site of Special Scientific Interest designation; arriving at the threshold, shrouded in an atmosphere of protection and attention sheltering the river and the Ings.

If they were not there, the birds would be in trouble.

This year, results from tracking another three whimbrels has further reinforced their dependence on specific sites; also eleven birds ringed here in 2006, were recaptured at the same place in 2007. And satellite records of the newly tagged whimbrels have returned readings not only from breeding grounds in Iceland, to which the individual travelled in just 36 hours, but from another breeding area on the Swedish/Finnish border.

But what does the future hold? If the last four decades are anything to go by, nothing can be taken for granted. To corrupt a well-known saying: the "Price of freedom, and conservation, is eternal vigilance".

Meanwhile, oblivious to our whims and fancies, plans and projects, the River Derwent rolls on. It is still one of Britain's loveliest rivers. It still snakes through secret tree-fringed gorges and quiet meadows. It is still unexploited and still very clean. We can only hope that it will stay that way.

David Ainger, the barrister in the River Derwent Court Case, beautifully summed up the justification for of all the endeavours, recounting a few well-chosen words of wisdom "It is said, that where fish are content, everything is in good order". To that I would add the birds and other wildlife. And I hope, just maybe, that whatever the future has in store, they are content along the Yorkshire River Derwent. At least for this Moment in Time.

The Derwent Song

By Margaret Wolstenholme

Who am I? What am I? Where am I going?
How can I live like a leaf on the breeze?
The arrow is loose and the fox is a running;
The price that I pay is the price to be free.

Sun am I, rain am I, river flowing
Under the boughs through the forests and Ings.
Stag am I, butterfly, seed I am sowing,
I'm the past and the future,
It's hope that I bring.

I am part of the acres of summer
Which from the ages of winter awoke.
Bird song and heartsease,
My light grows the stronger,
Just like the acorn and its mighty oak.

Come to me, cleave to me, love me and cherish
A vision of England with glades dappled green.
A hawk in the rain and a hare in the meadow,
Don't let me be lost to just legend or dream.

As the twilight falls on this green Eden,
Wrought by man's hand but with God standing near,
Darkened and still now, this peace of the ancients
Grows rarer and rarer with each passing year.

Come to me, cleave to me, love me and cherish
A vision of England with glades dappled green.
A hawk in the rain and a hare in the meadow,
Don't let me be lost to just legend or dream.

Postscript

At the outset of The Yorkshire River Derwent – Moments in Time the rejection by Parliament of a scheme to build a reservoir in Farndale in the North York Moors lay at the root of the recent phase of the Derwent's story.

While checking dates and facts on the Internet at the completion of the text, I chanced upon a 2006 article by Christine McCulloch, which explored the passage and failure of the Yorkshire Derwent Water Bill to authorise the making of the reservoir as it progressed through the House of Commons. Containing information only relatively recently open to the public under the thirty-year rule, it made astonishing reading.

In short, in 1970 approval by Parliament of a reservoir in Farndale seemed inevitable. Since the 1930s Kingston Upon Hull Corporation had the benefit of an Act of Parliament to enable its construction. But a fresh Act had been felt necessary to deal with the new proposals.

At the Second Reading, the River Derwent Water Bill passed by a large majority of 163 votes in favour to 61 votes against. However, in the Select Committee stage, which followed, when five MPs met to scrutinise the preamble – the evidence – for the need for the Bill, an extraordinary move took place.

Behind closed doors, after three days of debate a protocol was invoked, that any member of the Committee who had already voted in the House at the Second Reading and thus revealed their preferences, could not vote in the Committee. According to the article, this eliminated three of the members of the committee, reducing it to two, including the Chairman, Sir Samuel Knox Cunningham. The remaining Committee member voted for the reservoir, the Chairman against, and the Chairman then used his casting vote and the Farndale scheme was dead. The Bill had not been proven.

On such a slender thread perhaps all our histories hang.

Lucky charms: The otter skull, Alexander's woolly hat, a pair of child's plastic sunglasses, a golf ball kicked out of an entrance hole by a badger in the middle of the night, and the plastic pot which held the lucky Derwent water.

Abbreviations

BC	British Coal
CCT	Carstairs Countryside Trust
CONSYDER	Conservation Society for the Yorkshire Derwent
ECPT	Ellerton Church Preservation Trust
EA	Environment Agency
EN	English Nature
ERYC	East Riding of Yorkshire Council
HCC	Humberside County Council
HLF	Heritage Lottery Fund
LDCG	Lower Derwent Conservation Group
LGWT	Last Great Wetlands Trust
LOT	Light Owler Trust
NCB	National Coal Board
NCC	Nature Conservancy Council
NE	Natural England
NHMF	National Heritage Memorial Fund
NYCC	North Yorkshire County Council
RJB	RJB Mining (UK) Limited
RSPB	Royal Society for the Protection of Birds
UKC	UKCoal Limited
YNT	Yorkshire Naturalists Trust
YWT	Yorkshire Wildlife Trust
WAYD	Wildlife Association of the Yorkshire Derwent
WWF	World Wildlife Fund
WWFN	World Wide Fund For Nature
YDT	Yorkshire Derwent Trust Ltd
YW	Yorkshire Water

Name changes

East Riding of Yorkshire County Council (ERYC); part of Humberside County Council (HCC) 1974; reverted to East Riding of Yorkshire Council (ERYC) 1996.

Last Great Wetlands Trust (LGWT); to The Light Owler Trust (LOT) 2000.

National Coal Board (NCB); to British Coal (BC) 1997; privatised to RJB Mining (UK) Ltd (RJB) 1994; to UKCoal.

Nature Conservancy Council (NCC); to English Nature (EN) 1990; then Natural England (NE) 2006.

World Wildlife Fund (WWF); to World Wide Fund For Nature (WWFN) 1986.

Yorkshire Naturalist Trust (YNT); to The Yorkshire Wildlife Trust (YWT) 1983.

Conservation designations for land

NNR	National Nature Reserve
SSSI	Site of Special Scientific Interest
SAC	European Union Special Area of Conservation
SPA	European Union Special Protection Area for Birds
SM	Scheduled Monument
Ramsar Site	A Ramsar wetland of International Importance, named after a convention held in Ramsar, Iran.

The Author

Born in Perthshire, Ian Carstairs moved to Surrey, then to Yorkshire and he now divides his time between living in Malton, North Yorkshire and Harleston in South Norfolk.

Ian co-ordinated the River Derwent Campaign for the River Derwent Group and acted as 'honest broker' to negotiate a solution to the Review of the Selby Coalfield Planning Consent, under EU Habitats Directive Regulations. He was the founding trustee of the Carstairs Countryside Trust, a conservation charity.

After training as a graphic designer and photographer at Epsom School of Art in Surrey, Ian changed careers when he became assistant Director of the Moors Centre in the Esk Valley, before embarking on self-employment and becoming involved with major wildlife and countryside projects.

Formal roles followed, firstly as a Secretary of State's Appointed Member to the Board of the North York Moors National Park Authority, concluding his appointment as Deputy Chairman. A spell on the England Committee of the Heritage Lottery fund preceded Chairmanship of the Yorkshire and The Humber Committee, when the HLF regionalised its operations. He has also been a member of both the National Rivers Authority and Forestry Commission's Regional Advisory Committees.

Ian has been the author and photographer of a number of books including: A Portrait of York, A Portrait of Hull, Moods of the Yorkshire Coast, Moods of the North York Moors, A Harvest of Colour – Saving Cornfield Flowers and the official guide to The North York Moors National Park.

He was made an MBE for services to conservation in 1995 and an OBE for Services to the Heritage in 2007. He was also awarded the National Federation of Anglers' Gold Medal for meritorious service to the conservation of rivers and received The Golden Scale, the Mark of the Golden Scale Club for his work on the Yorkshire Derwent

Chairman of the Light Owler Trust, Ian cares passionately about the Derwent and the quality of the countryside and the need to maintain a sense of humour and occasion.

From a hundreds-of-years-old newt carved into Aughton church tower to a fleeting image of a fragile and ephemeral shed newt skin floating on the water, like a constellation in the sky – the very spirit of the River Derwent and its Ings.